55 Northwestern States Recipes for Home

By: Kelly Johnson

Table of Contents

- Pacific Northwest Salmon Bake (Washington/Oregon)
- Idaho Potato Soup (Idaho)
- Montana Huckleberry Pie (Montana)
- Oregon Hazelnut Pesto Pasta (Oregon)
- Washington Apple Crisp (Washington)
- Northwestern Clam Chowder (Regional)
- Wild Mushroom Risotto (Northwestern Forests)
- Salmon and Berry Salad (Alaska and Pacific Northwest)
- Grilled Idaho Trout with Lemon and Herbs (Idaho)
- Northwestern Veggie Skewers (Regional)
- Oregon Dungeness Crab Cakes (Oregon)
- Idaho Finger Steaks (Idaho)
- Washington Cherry Chicken Salad (Washington)
- Montana Bison Chili (Montana)
- Northwestern Grilled Veggie Pizza (Regional)
- Smoked Salmon Bagels with Cream Cheese (Alaska/Washington)
- Idaho Huckleberry BBQ Sauce (Idaho)
- Oregon Marionberry BBQ Chicken (Oregon)
- Montana Bison Burger with Wild Mushroom Sauce (Montana)
- Northwestern Quinoa Salad (Regional)
- Alaska Halibut Tacos with Mango Salsa (Alaska)
- Washington Apple and Gorgonzola Stuffed CHicken Breast (Washington)
- Oregon Pinot Noir Braised Short Ribs (Oregon)
- Idaho Trout with Lemon-Dill Sauce (Idaho)
- Montana Huckleberry Pancakes (Montana)
- Northwestern Quiche with Smoked Salmon and Asparagus (Regional)
- Washington Cherry Balsamic Glazed Pork Chops (Washington)
- Alaska King Crab Linguine (Alaska)
- Idaho Potato Gnocchi with Sage Butter (Idaho)
- Northwestern Berry Cobbler (Regional)
- Oregon Hazelnut-Crusted Tilapia (Oregon)
- Washington Potato Leek Soup (Washington)
- Idaho Sun-Dried Tomato and Basil Stuffed Chicken (Idaho)
- Montana Bison and Barley Soup (Montana)
- Alaska Smoked Salmon and Avocado Salad (Alaska)
- Northwestern Wild Mushroom and Spinach Frittata (Regional)

- Washington Apple and Cheddar Grilled Cheese (Washington)
- Idaho Potato and Chorizo Breakfast Burritos (Idaho)
- Oregon Marionberry Sorbet (Oregon)
- Northwestern Lox and Bagel Brunch Board (Regional)
- Alaska Halibut Chowder (Alaska)
- Washington Apple Walnut Salad (Washington)
- Idaho Sage and Honey Glazed CHicken (Idaho)
- Oregon Marionberry BBQ Pulled Pork Sliders (Oregon)
- Montana Huckleberry Cheesecake Bars (Montana)

Pacific Northwest Salmon Bake (Washington/Oregon)

Ingredients:

- 4 salmon fillets (wild-caught Pacific salmon)
- 1/4 cup olive oil
- 3 tablespoons Dijon mustard
- 3 tablespoons maple syrup
- 2 tablespoons soy sauce
- 2 cloves garlic, minced
- 1 teaspoon smoked paprika
- 1 teaspoon dried thyme
- Salt and pepper, to taste
- Lemon wedges for serving

Instructions:

Preheat the Oven:
- Preheat your oven to 400°F (200°C).

Prepare the Marinade:
- In a small bowl, whisk together the olive oil, Dijon mustard, maple syrup, soy sauce, minced garlic, smoked paprika, dried thyme, salt, and pepper. This creates a flavorful marinade for the salmon.

Marinate the Salmon:
- Place the salmon fillets in a shallow dish or a resealable plastic bag. Pour the marinade over the salmon, making sure to coat each fillet evenly. Allow it to marinate for at least 30 minutes in the refrigerator. For a more intense flavor, you can marinate it for up to 2 hours.

Prepare Baking Dish:
- Grease a baking dish lightly or line it with parchment paper.

Bake the Salmon:
- Place the marinated salmon fillets in the prepared baking dish. Bake in the preheated oven for about 15-20 minutes, or until the salmon easily flakes with a fork. The cooking time may vary based on the thickness of your fillets.

Broil for Crispy Top (Optional):
- If you prefer a slightly crispy top, you can broil the salmon for an additional 2-3 minutes at the end. Keep an eye on it to prevent burning.

Serve:
- Remove the salmon from the oven and let it rest for a few minutes. Serve the salmon with lemon wedges for a fresh citrusy flavor.

Garnish (Optional):

- Garnish with fresh herbs like chopped parsley or dill for a burst of color and added freshness.

This Pacific Northwest Salmon Bake captures the essence of the region's seafood and combines it with a flavorful marinade that enhances the natural taste of the salmon. Enjoy your delicious and locally-inspired meal!

Idaho Potato Soup (Idaho)

Ingredients:

- 4 large Idaho potatoes, peeled and diced
- 1 large onion, finely chopped
- 2 cloves garlic, minced
- 4 cups chicken or vegetable broth
- 1 cup whole milk
- 1/2 cup heavy cream (optional, for a creamier soup)
- 4 tablespoons unsalted butter
- 1/4 cup all-purpose flour
- Salt and pepper, to taste
- 1 cup shredded sharp cheddar cheese
- Chives or green onions, chopped (for garnish)
- Crispy bacon bits (optional, for garnish)
- Sour cream (optional, for serving)

Instructions:

Prepare Potatoes:
- Peel and dice the Idaho potatoes into small cubes, ensuring they are relatively uniform in size for even cooking.

Sauté Onion and Garlic:
- In a large pot, melt 2 tablespoons of butter over medium heat. Add chopped onions and minced garlic, sautéing until softened and fragrant.

Make Roux:
- Add the remaining 2 tablespoons of butter to the pot. Once melted, sprinkle in the flour, stirring constantly to create a roux. Cook for 2-3 minutes to eliminate the raw flour taste.

Add Broth and Potatoes:
- Gradually whisk in the chicken or vegetable broth, ensuring there are no lumps. Add the diced potatoes to the pot and bring the mixture to a simmer. Let it cook until the potatoes are tender (about 15-20 minutes).

Blend Soup (Optional):
- For a creamier texture, use an immersion blender to partially blend the soup. You can also transfer a portion of the soup to a blender, blend until smooth, and then return it to the pot.

Add Milk and Cream:
- Pour in the whole milk and heavy cream (if using). Stir well and let the soup simmer for an additional 5-10 minutes.

Season and Add Cheese:

- Season the soup with salt and pepper to taste. Stir in the shredded cheddar cheese until melted and well incorporated.

Serve:
- Ladle the Idaho Potato Soup into bowls. Garnish with chopped chives or green onions, crispy bacon bits (if desired), and a dollop of sour cream.

Enjoy:
- Serve the soup hot and enjoy the comforting flavors of this Idaho-inspired potato soup.

This Idaho Potato Soup is rich, creamy, and highlights the deliciousness of Idaho's famous potatoes. Enjoy your warm and hearty bowl!

Montana Huckleberry Pie (Montana)

Ingredients:

For the Pie Crust:

- 2 1/2 cups all-purpose flour
- 1 cup unsalted butter, cold and diced
- 1 teaspoon salt
- 1 tablespoon granulated sugar
- 1/4 to 1/2 cup ice water

For the Huckleberry Filling:

- 4 cups fresh huckleberries, cleaned and stems removed
- 3/4 cup granulated sugar (adjust based on the sweetness of the berries)
- 1/4 cup cornstarch
- 1 tablespoon lemon juice
- Zest of one lemon
- 1/4 teaspoon cinnamon (optional)

For Assembly:

- 1 tablespoon milk (for brushing the crust)
- 1 tablespoon granulated sugar (for sprinkling)

Instructions:

Prepare the Pie Crust:

   Combine Ingredients:
   - In a large bowl, combine the flour, salt, and sugar. Add the cold, diced butter. Using a pastry cutter or your hands, work the butter into the flour until the mixture resembles coarse crumbs.

   Add Water:
   - Gradually add the ice water, one tablespoon at a time, and mix until the dough just comes together. Be careful not to overmix. Form the dough into a disc, wrap it in plastic wrap, and refrigerate for at least 1 hour.

   Roll Out Crust:

- Preheat your oven to 375°F (190°C). On a floured surface, roll out the chilled dough to fit a 9-inch pie dish. Transfer the crust to the dish, trim any excess, and crimp the edges.

Prepare the Huckleberry Filling:

Mix Ingredients:
- In a large bowl, gently mix the huckleberries, sugar, cornstarch, lemon juice, lemon zest, and cinnamon (if using). Ensure the berries are evenly coated.

Assemble and Bake:

Fill the Crust:
- Pour the huckleberry filling into the prepared pie crust.

Top with Second Crust:
- Roll out the remaining dough for the top crust. You can create a lattice design or cover the pie with a full crust. Trim and crimp the edges. If you're doing a full crust, cut a few slits to allow steam to escape.

Brush with Milk and Sprinkle Sugar:
- Brush the top crust with a bit of milk and sprinkle sugar over it for a golden finish.

Bake:
- Place the pie on a baking sheet to catch any drips. Bake for 45-55 minutes or until the crust is golden and the filling is bubbly.

Cool:
- Allow the pie to cool on a wire rack before serving. This helps the filling set.

Serve and Enjoy:
- Serve slices of Montana Huckleberry Pie on their own or with a scoop of vanilla ice cream for a delicious treat!

This Montana Huckleberry Pie is a delightful way to savor the unique and delicious taste of huckleberries. Enjoy!

Oregon Hazelnut Pesto Pasta (Oregon)

Ingredients:

For the Hazelnut Pesto:

- 1 cup fresh basil leaves, packed
- 1/2 cup Oregon hazelnuts, toasted and skins removed
- 1/2 cup grated Parmesan cheese
- 2 cloves garlic, peeled
- 1/2 cup extra-virgin olive oil
- Salt and pepper, to taste
- Juice of half a lemon

For the Pasta:

- 12 ounces (about 350g) of your favorite pasta (spaghetti, fettuccine, or any shape you prefer)
- Salt, for boiling pasta
- Cherry tomatoes, halved (optional, for garnish)
- Extra grated Parmesan cheese, for serving
- Fresh basil leaves, for garnish

Instructions:

Prepare Hazelnut Pesto:

Toast Hazelnuts:
- Preheat your oven to 350°F (175°C). Spread hazelnuts on a baking sheet and toast in the oven for about 10 minutes, or until fragrant. Allow them to cool slightly and then rub off the skins using a clean kitchen towel.

Make Pesto:
- In a food processor, combine the toasted hazelnuts, basil, Parmesan cheese, and garlic. Pulse until finely chopped.

Stream in Olive Oil:
- With the food processor running, gradually stream in the olive oil until the pesto reaches your desired consistency. Season with salt and pepper to taste. Squeeze in the lemon juice and pulse once more to combine.

Prepare Pasta:

Cook Pasta:
- Cook the pasta according to package instructions in a large pot of salted boiling water until al dente. Reserve about a cup of pasta water before draining.

Combine with Pesto:
- In a large bowl, toss the cooked pasta with the hazelnut pesto, using some of the reserved pasta water to achieve a creamy consistency.

Garnish:
- Garnish with halved cherry tomatoes, extra grated Parmesan cheese, and fresh basil leaves.

Serve:
- Serve the Oregon Hazelnut Pesto Pasta immediately, drizzling with a bit more olive oil if desired. Enjoy the flavors of Oregon in this delightful and nutty pesto pasta!

This Oregon Hazelnut Pesto Pasta is a delicious way to showcase the distinctive taste of hazelnuts and the vibrant culinary scene of the state. Enjoy your meal!

Washington Apple Crisp (Washington)

Ingredients:

For the Apple Filling:

- 6 cups Washington apples, peeled, cored, and thinly sliced (a mix of sweet and tart varieties like Honeycrisp and Granny Smith works well)
- 1/2 cup granulated sugar
- 1 tablespoon all-purpose flour
- 1 teaspoon ground cinnamon
- 1/4 teaspoon ground nutmeg
- 1 tablespoon lemon juice

For the Crisp Topping:

- 1 cup old-fashioned rolled oats
- 1/2 cup all-purpose flour
- 1/2 cup packed light brown sugar
- 1/4 teaspoon salt
- 1/2 cup unsalted butter, cold and diced

Optional Garnish:

- Vanilla ice cream or whipped cream

Instructions:

Prepare the Apple Filling:

    Preheat Oven:
- Preheat your oven to 350°F (175°C).

    Slice Apples:
- Peel, core, and thinly slice the Washington apples.

    Mix Ingredients:
- In a large bowl, combine the sliced apples with granulated sugar, flour, cinnamon, nutmeg, and lemon juice. Toss until the apples are evenly coated.

Prepare the Crisp Topping:

Combine Dry Ingredients:
- In another bowl, combine rolled oats, flour, brown sugar, and salt.

Add Butter:
- Add the cold, diced butter to the dry ingredients. Using your fingers or a pastry cutter, work the butter into the mixture until it resembles coarse crumbs.

Assemble and Bake:

Layer in Baking Dish:
- Grease a baking dish (9x13 inches or a similar size) and spread the apple mixture evenly across the bottom.

Sprinkle Topping:
- Sprinkle the crisp topping evenly over the apples, covering them completely.

Bake:
- Bake in the preheated oven for 40-45 minutes or until the topping is golden brown, and the apples are tender and bubbly.

Cool:
- Allow the Washington Apple Crisp to cool for a few minutes before serving.

Serve:

Optional Garnish:
- Serve warm, either on its own or with a scoop of vanilla ice cream or a dollop of whipped cream.

Enjoy:
- Enjoy the delicious flavors of Washington apples in this comforting and easy-to-make apple crisp!

This Washington Apple Crisp is a perfect way to celebrate the delightful sweetness of Washington-grown apples. Feel free to adjust the sugar and spice levels based on your taste preferences. Enjoy your delicious dessert!

Northwestern Clam Chowder (Regional)

Ingredients:

- 4 slices bacon, chopped
- 1 onion, finely diced
- 2 celery stalks, finely diced
- 2 carrots, peeled and finely diced
- 2 cloves garlic, minced
- 3 tablespoons all-purpose flour
- 4 cups Yukon Gold potatoes, peeled and diced
- 3 cups clam juice (from canned clams)
- 1 bay leaf
- 1 teaspoon dried thyme
- 1/2 teaspoon dried oregano
- 1/2 teaspoon smoked paprika
- Salt and black pepper, to taste
- 2 cups whole milk
- 1 cup heavy cream
- 2 cans (6.5 oz each) chopped clams, drained
- Fresh parsley, chopped, for garnish
- Oyster crackers or crusty bread, for serving

Instructions:

Prepare the Chowder Base:

Cook Bacon:
- In a large pot, cook the chopped bacon over medium heat until it becomes crispy. Remove some bacon bits for garnish and leave some in the pot for flavor.

Sauté Vegetables:
- Add diced onion, celery, carrots, and minced garlic to the pot. Sauté until the vegetables are softened.

Add Flour:
- Sprinkle the flour over the sautéed vegetables and bacon. Stir continuously to create a roux and cook for 2-3 minutes.

Add Potatoes and Liquids:
- Add diced potatoes, clam juice, bay leaf, dried thyme, dried oregano, smoked paprika, salt, and black pepper. Stir well.

Simmer:
- Bring the mixture to a simmer and let it cook until the potatoes are tender, stirring occasionally.

Finish the Chowder:

Add Milk and Cream:
- Pour in the whole milk and heavy cream. Stir to combine and let the chowder simmer for an additional 10-15 minutes.

Add Clams:
- Gently fold in the drained chopped clams. Cook for an additional 5 minutes until the clams are heated through.

Adjust Seasoning:
- Taste and adjust salt and pepper as needed. Remove the bay leaf.

Serve:

Garnish and Serve:
- Ladle the Northwestern Clam Chowder into bowls. Garnish with reserved crispy bacon bits and chopped fresh parsley.

Serve Warm:
- Serve the clam chowder warm with oyster crackers or crusty bread on the side.

This Northwestern Clam Chowder is a comforting and hearty dish, perfect for enjoying the flavors of the region. Enjoy your bowl of creamy, flavorful chowder!

Wild Mushroom Risotto (Northwestern Forests)

Ingredients:

- 1 1/2 cups Arborio rice
- 1/2 cup dry white wine
- 6 cups vegetable or chicken broth, kept warm
- 1/2 cup shallots, finely chopped
- 2 cloves garlic, minced
- 1/2 cup Parmesan cheese, grated
- 1/4 cup unsalted butter
- 2 tablespoons olive oil
- 1 pound assorted wild mushrooms (such as chanterelles, morels, shiitake), cleaned and sliced
- 1/2 cup fresh parsley, chopped
- Salt and black pepper, to taste

Instructions:

Prepare the Mushrooms:

Sauté Mushrooms:
- In a large pan, heat 1 tablespoon of olive oil over medium heat. Add the sliced wild mushrooms and sauté until they release their moisture and become golden brown. Season with salt and pepper. Set aside.

Make the Risotto:

Sauté Shallots and Garlic:
- In a large, heavy-bottomed pot, heat the remaining olive oil over medium heat. Add the chopped shallots and garlic. Sauté until softened.

Toast Rice:
- Add Arborio rice to the pot, stirring to coat the rice in the oil, shallots, and garlic. Toast the rice for about 2 minutes until it becomes slightly translucent at the edges.

Deglaze with Wine:
- Pour in the dry white wine, stirring constantly until the wine is mostly absorbed by the rice.

Add Broth:

- Begin adding the warm broth to the rice one ladle at a time, stirring frequently. Allow the liquid to be mostly absorbed before adding the next ladle. Continue this process until the rice is creamy and cooked to al dente, about 18-20 minutes.

Finish Risotto:
- Stir in the sautéed wild mushrooms, Parmesan cheese, and butter. Mix until the cheese and butter are melted, and the mushrooms are evenly distributed throughout the risotto.

Adjust Seasoning:
- Taste the risotto and adjust the seasoning with salt and black pepper as needed.

Serve:

Garnish and Serve:
- Garnish the Wild Mushroom Risotto with fresh chopped parsley. Serve immediately, ensuring the risotto is hot and creamy.

This Northwestern Wild Mushroom Risotto is a luxurious and earthy dish that captures the essence of the region's forests. Enjoy the rich flavors and creamy texture of this delightful risotto!

Salmon and Berry Salad (Alaska and Pacific Northwest)

Ingredients:

For the Salmon:

- 1 pound fresh salmon fillets
- 1 tablespoon olive oil
- Salt and black pepper, to taste
- 1 teaspoon smoked paprika
- 1 teaspoon lemon zest

For the Salad:

- 6 cups mixed salad greens (e.g., spinach, arugula, and watercress)
- 1 cup fresh blueberries
- 1 cup fresh raspberries
- 1 cup sliced strawberries
- 1/2 cup crumbled feta cheese
- 1/4 cup chopped fresh mint

For the Dressing:

- 3 tablespoons extra-virgin olive oil
- 2 tablespoons balsamic vinegar
- 1 tablespoon honey
- Salt and black pepper, to taste

Instructions:

Prepare the Salmon:

Preheat Oven:
- Preheat your oven to 400°F (200°C).

Season Salmon:
- Place the salmon fillets on a baking sheet lined with parchment paper. Drizzle with olive oil and season with salt, black pepper, smoked paprika, and lemon zest.

Bake Salmon:

- Bake in the preheated oven for 12-15 minutes or until the salmon is cooked through and easily flakes with a fork. Cooking time may vary based on the thickness of the fillets. Once done, let the salmon cool slightly.

Flake Salmon:
- Flake the cooked salmon into bite-sized pieces.

Assemble the Salad:

Prepare Salad Greens:
- In a large salad bowl, combine the mixed greens.

Add Berries and Cheese:
- Add the fresh blueberries, raspberries, sliced strawberries, and crumbled feta cheese to the salad greens.

Add Flaked Salmon:
- Gently mix in the flaked salmon, distributing it evenly throughout the salad.

Make the Dressing:

Whisk Dressing:
- In a small bowl, whisk together the extra-virgin olive oil, balsamic vinegar, honey, salt, and black pepper. Adjust the sweetness and acidity to your liking.

Serve:

Drizzle Dressing:
- Drizzle the dressing over the salad just before serving.

Garnish:
- Garnish the Salmon and Berry Salad with chopped fresh mint.

Serve Immediately:
- Serve the salad immediately for the best freshness and flavor.

This Salmon and Berry Salad is a delightful combination of nutritious greens, succulent salmon, and the sweet burst of berries. Enjoy this wholesome and vibrant dish inspired by the Pacific Northwest!

Grilled Idaho Trout with Lemon and Herbs (Idaho)

Ingredients:

- 4 whole Idaho trout, cleaned and gutted
- 1/4 cup fresh lemon juice
- 2 tablespoons olive oil
- 2 cloves garlic, minced
- 2 tablespoons fresh parsley, finely chopped
- 1 tablespoon fresh dill, finely chopped
- Salt and black pepper, to taste
- Lemon slices, for garnish
- Fresh herbs (parsley, dill) for garnish

Instructions:

Prepare the Marinade:

Whisk Marinade Ingredients:
- In a small bowl, whisk together the fresh lemon juice, olive oil, minced garlic, chopped parsley, chopped dill, salt, and black pepper. This will be your marinade.

Prepare the Trout:

Clean and Pat Dry:
- Ensure the trout are thoroughly cleaned and patted dry with paper towels.

Marinate the Trout:
- Place the trout in a shallow dish or a large resealable plastic bag. Pour the marinade over the trout, making sure to coat each fish evenly. Allow it to marinate for at least 30 minutes in the refrigerator. For a more intense flavor, you can marinate it for up to 2 hours.

Grill the Trout:

Preheat the Grill:
- Preheat your grill to medium-high heat.

Oil the Grates:
- Brush the grill grates with a bit of oil to prevent sticking.

Grill Trout:

- Place the marinated trout on the preheated grill. Grill for about 4-6 minutes per side, or until the flesh easily flakes with a fork. Cooking time may vary based on the size of the trout.

Baste with Marinade:
- Occasionally baste the trout with some of the marinade while grilling to enhance the flavors.

Garnish:
- Once the trout is grilled to perfection, remove it from the grill. Garnish with fresh lemon slices and additional chopped herbs.

Serve:

Serve Hot:
- Serve the Grilled Idaho Trout immediately while it's hot, accompanied by your favorite side dishes.

This Grilled Idaho Trout with Lemon and Herbs is a fantastic way to enjoy the fresh and delicate flavors of trout, enhanced by the zesty lemon and aromatic herbs. It's a perfect dish to celebrate the bounty of Idaho. Enjoy your delicious and grilled-to-perfection trout!

Northwestern Veggie Skewers (Regional)

Ingredients:

- 1 large red bell pepper, cut into chunks
- 1 large yellow bell pepper, cut into chunks
- 1 large red onion, cut into chunks
- 1 zucchini, sliced into rounds
- 1 yellow squash, sliced into rounds
- Cherry tomatoes
- Button mushrooms, cleaned
- 1/4 cup extra-virgin olive oil
- 2 tablespoons balsamic vinegar
- 2 cloves garlic, minced
- 1 teaspoon dried oregano
- Salt and black pepper, to taste
- Fresh parsley, chopped, for garnish

Instructions:

Prepare the Marinade:

Whisk Marinade Ingredients:
- In a small bowl, whisk together the extra-virgin olive oil, balsamic vinegar, minced garlic, dried oregano, salt, and black pepper. This will be your marinade.

Prepare the Veggie Skewers:

Soak Skewers:
- If you're using wooden skewers, soak them in water for about 30 minutes to prevent burning during grilling.

Assemble Skewers:
- Thread the chunks of red and yellow bell peppers, red onion, zucchini, yellow squash, cherry tomatoes, and button mushrooms onto the skewers, alternating the vegetables for a colorful presentation.

Brush with Marinade:
- Place the assembled veggie skewers in a shallow dish and brush them with the prepared marinade, ensuring all the vegetables are well-coated. Allow them to marinate for at least 15-20 minutes.

Grill the Veggie Skewers:

- Preheat the Grill:
  - Preheat your grill to medium-high heat.
- Oil the Grates:
  - Brush the grill grates with a bit of oil to prevent sticking.
- Grill Skewers:
  - Place the veggie skewers on the preheated grill. Grill for about 8-10 minutes, turning occasionally, or until the vegetables are tender and have a nice char.
- Baste with Marinade:
  - Baste the skewers with the remaining marinade while grilling to enhance the flavors.

Serve:

- Garnish and Serve:
  - Remove the Northwestern Veggie Skewers from the grill and garnish with chopped fresh parsley. Serve immediately as a delicious and colorful side dish or as a vegetarian main course.

These Northwestern Veggie Skewers are a wonderful way to celebrate the vibrant and diverse flavors of the region. Enjoy the freshness and goodness of the grilled vegetables!

Oregon Dungeness Crab Cakes (Oregon)

Ingredients:

- 1 pound Dungeness crab meat, picked through for shells
- 1/2 cup breadcrumbs (plus extra for coating)
- 1/4 cup mayonnaise
- 2 tablespoons Dijon mustard
- 2 green onions, finely chopped
- 1/4 cup red bell pepper, finely diced
- 1/4 cup fresh parsley, chopped
- 1 large egg, beaten
- 1 teaspoon Worcestershire sauce
- 1 teaspoon Old Bay seasoning
- Salt and black pepper, to taste
- Olive oil, for frying
- Lemon wedges, for serving

Instructions:

Prepare Crab Mixture:
- In a large mixing bowl, combine the Dungeness crab meat, breadcrumbs, mayonnaise, Dijon mustard, green onions, red bell pepper, parsley, beaten egg, Worcestershire sauce, Old Bay seasoning, salt, and black pepper. Gently fold the ingredients together until well combined.

Form Crab Cakes:
- Divide the crab mixture into equal portions and shape them into crab cakes. Coat each crab cake with additional breadcrumbs for a crispy exterior.

Chill Crab Cakes:
- Place the formed crab cakes on a baking sheet and refrigerate for at least 30 minutes. Chilling helps them firm up and hold their shape during cooking.

Preheat Oven:
- Preheat your oven to 200°F (93°C) to keep the crab cakes warm while cooking batches.

Fry Crab Cakes:
- In a large skillet, heat olive oil over medium heat. Carefully place the crab cakes in the hot oil and cook for about 4-5 minutes per side, or until they are golden brown and cooked through.

Drain and Keep Warm:
- Once cooked, transfer the crab cakes to a paper towel-lined plate to drain any excess oil. Place them in the preheated oven to keep warm while you cook the remaining batches.

Serve:
- Serve the Oregon Dungeness Crab Cakes warm, garnished with fresh parsley and accompanied by lemon wedges for squeezing.

These Oregon Dungeness Crab Cakes are a delightful treat, showcasing the delicious and delicate flavor of Dungeness crab. Enjoy them as an appetizer, a light lunch, or part of a seafood feast!

Idaho Finger Steaks (Idaho)

Ingredients:

For the Marinade:

- 1 pound beef sirloin or round steak, thinly sliced into strips
- 1 cup buttermilk
- 1 teaspoon hot sauce (adjust to taste)
- 1 teaspoon garlic powder
- 1 teaspoon onion powder
- Salt and black pepper, to taste

For the Coating:

- 1 cup all-purpose flour
- 1 teaspoon paprika
- 1 teaspoon garlic powder
- 1 teaspoon onion powder
- Salt and black pepper, to taste

For Frying:

- Vegetable oil, for frying

Instructions:

Prepare the Marinade:

Marinate Beef:
- In a bowl, combine the thinly sliced beef strips with buttermilk, hot sauce, garlic powder, onion powder, salt, and black pepper. Ensure the beef is well coated. Marinate in the refrigerator for at least 2 hours, or preferably overnight.

Coat and Fry the Finger Steaks:

Prepare Coating:
- In a shallow dish, combine the all-purpose flour, paprika, garlic powder, onion powder, salt, and black pepper. Mix well to create the coating mixture.

Coat the Beef Strips:
- Remove the marinated beef strips from the buttermilk mixture, allowing any excess to drip off. Dredge the strips in the coating mixture, pressing the flour mixture onto the beef to ensure a good coating.

Heat Oil:
- In a deep skillet or frying pan, heat enough vegetable oil for frying over medium-high heat. The oil should be around 350°F (175°C).

Fry Finger Steaks:
- Carefully place the coated beef strips into the hot oil, making sure not to overcrowd the pan. Fry for 2-3 minutes per side or until the coating is golden brown and the beef is cooked to your liking.

Drain and Rest:
- Remove the finger steaks from the oil and place them on a paper towel-lined plate to drain any excess oil. Let them rest for a few minutes.

Serve:

Garnish and Enjoy:
- Serve the Idaho Finger Steaks hot as an appetizer or main dish. Garnish with your favorite dipping sauce or serve with fries for a complete Idaho-inspired meal.

These Idaho Finger Steaks are crispy on the outside and tender on the inside, making them a delightful and flavorful dish that showcases the culinary traditions of Idaho. Enjoy your tasty finger steaks!

Washington Cherry Chicken Salad (Washington)

Ingredients:

For the Salad:

- 2 cups cooked and shredded chicken (rotisserie chicken works well)
- 1 cup fresh Washington cherries, pitted and halved
- 1/2 cup celery, finely chopped
- 1/4 cup red onion, finely chopped
- 1/2 cup walnuts or pecans, chopped
- Mixed salad greens (e.g., arugula, spinach, or your favorite greens)

For the Dressing:

- 1/4 cup mayonnaise
- 2 tablespoons Greek yogurt
- 1 tablespoon Dijon mustard
- 1 tablespoon honey
- 1 tablespoon apple cider vinegar
- Salt and black pepper, to taste

Optional Garnish:

- Crumbled feta or goat cheese
- Fresh mint leaves, chopped

Instructions:

Prepare the Salad:

Cook and Shred Chicken:
- Cook and shred the chicken. You can use rotisserie chicken or cook chicken breasts and shred them.

Combine Salad Ingredients:
- In a large bowl, combine the shredded chicken, halved Washington cherries, chopped celery, red onion, and chopped nuts.

Prepare the Dressing:

Whisk Dressing:

- In a small bowl, whisk together mayonnaise, Greek yogurt, Dijon mustard, honey, apple cider vinegar, salt, and black pepper. Adjust the sweetness and acidity to your liking.

Dress the Salad:
- Pour the dressing over the salad ingredients and toss until everything is well coated.

Assemble and Serve:

Serve on Greens:
- Arrange a bed of mixed salad greens on individual plates or a serving platter.

Top with Cherry Chicken Salad:
- Spoon the cherry chicken salad mixture over the bed of salad greens.

Optional Garnish:
- If desired, sprinkle crumbled feta or goat cheese and chopped fresh mint leaves on top for added flavor.

Serve:
- Serve the Washington Cherry Chicken Salad immediately, offering extra dressing on the side if desired.

This Washington Cherry Chicken Salad is a delightful combination of sweet Washington cherries, savory chicken, and crunchy nuts. It's a perfect dish to enjoy during the summer months when cherries are in season. Enjoy your fresh and flavorful salad!

Montana Bison Chili (Montana)

Ingredients:

- 1 pound ground Montana bison meat
- 1 tablespoon olive oil
- 1 large onion, diced
- 3 cloves garlic, minced
- 1 bell pepper, diced (any color)
- 1 jalapeño, seeded and finely chopped (optional, for heat)
- 2 cans (15 oz each) kidney beans, drained and rinsed
- 1 can (28 oz) diced tomatoes, undrained
- 1 can (6 oz) tomato paste
- 2 cups beef or bison broth
- 2 tablespoons chili powder
- 1 tablespoon ground cumin
- 1 teaspoon smoked paprika
- 1 teaspoon dried oregano
- 1/2 teaspoon cayenne pepper (adjust to taste)
- Salt and black pepper, to taste
- Chopped fresh cilantro, for garnish
- Shredded cheddar cheese, for topping
- Sour cream, for serving
- Sliced green onions, for garnish

Instructions:

Cook Bison and Vegetables:

Brown Bison:
- In a large pot or Dutch oven, heat olive oil over medium-high heat. Add the ground bison and brown it, breaking it apart with a spoon as it cooks.

Add Aromatics:
- Add diced onions, minced garlic, diced bell pepper, and chopped jalapeño (if using). Sauté until the vegetables are softened.

Prepare Chili:

Combine Ingredients:

- Stir in kidney beans, diced tomatoes, tomato paste, beef or bison broth, chili powder, ground cumin, smoked paprika, dried oregano, cayenne pepper, salt, and black pepper.

Simmer:
- Bring the chili to a boil, then reduce the heat to low. Cover and let it simmer for at least 30 minutes to allow the flavors to meld. You can simmer for longer if you have the time.

Adjust Seasoning:
- Taste the chili and adjust the seasoning as needed. Add more chili powder, salt, or cayenne pepper if you prefer more heat.

Serve:

Garnish and Serve:
- Ladle the Montana Bison Chili into bowls. Garnish with chopped cilantro, shredded cheddar cheese, sour cream, and sliced green onions.

Enjoy:
- Serve the chili hot, perhaps with a side of crusty bread or cornbread. Enjoy the hearty and flavorful Montana Bison Chili!

This Montana Bison Chili is a robust and comforting dish, perfect for chilly days. The lean bison meat and a blend of spices create a savory and satisfying chili experience. Enjoy your bowl of Montana-inspired goodness!

Northwestern Grilled Veggie Pizza (Regional)

Ingredients:

For the Pizza Dough:

- 1 pound pizza dough (store-bought or homemade)
- Olive oil, for brushing

For the Pizza Sauce:

- 1/2 cup tomato sauce
- 2 cloves garlic, minced
- 1 teaspoon dried oregano
- Salt and black pepper, to taste

For the Grilled Veggies:

- 1 red bell pepper, sliced
- 1 yellow bell pepper, sliced
- 1 zucchini, thinly sliced
- 1 red onion, thinly sliced
- 1 cup cherry tomatoes, halved
- 1 cup cremini mushrooms, sliced
- 2 tablespoons olive oil
- Salt and black pepper, to taste
- 1 teaspoon dried thyme

For the Toppings:

- 1 cup shredded mozzarella cheese
- 1/2 cup crumbled feta cheese
- Fresh basil leaves, chopped, for garnish

Instructions:

Prepare the Grilled Veggies:

    Preheat Grill:
- Preheat your grill to medium-high heat.

    Toss Veggies:

- In a large bowl, toss the sliced bell peppers, zucchini, red onion, cherry tomatoes, and mushrooms with olive oil, salt, black pepper, and dried thyme.

Grill Veggies:
- Grill the veggies on the preheated grill until they have a nice char and are slightly softened. Remove from the grill and set aside.

Prepare the Pizza Dough:

Roll out Dough:
- On a lightly floured surface, roll out the pizza dough to your desired thickness.

Preheat Grill for Pizza:
- Preheat your grill to medium-high heat. Brush the grates with olive oil to prevent sticking.

Grill Pizza Dough:
- Carefully transfer the rolled-out pizza dough onto the preheated grill. Grill for 2-3 minutes on one side until it has grill marks, then flip.

Make Pizza Sauce:

Prepare Sauce:
- In a small bowl, mix together tomato sauce, minced garlic, dried oregano, salt, and black pepper.

Assemble the Pizza:

Spread Sauce:
- Spread the pizza sauce over the grilled side of the dough.

Add Cheese and Veggies:
- Sprinkle shredded mozzarella cheese over the sauce, then add the grilled veggies on top. Crumble feta cheese evenly over the pizza.

Finish Grilling:
- Close the grill lid and continue grilling for an additional 4-5 minutes, or until the cheese is melted, and the crust is golden brown.

Serve:

Garnish and Serve:

- Remove the Northwestern Grilled Veggie Pizza from the grill. Garnish with chopped fresh basil. Slice and serve hot.

This Northwestern Grilled Veggie Pizza is a celebration of fresh, regional produce, and the smoky flavors from the grill add an extra layer of deliciousness. Enjoy the taste of the Pacific Northwest in every bite!

Smoked Salmon Bagels with Cream Cheese (Alaska/Washington)

Ingredients:

- 4 bagels, sliced and toasted
- 8 ounces cream cheese, softened
- 8 ounces smoked salmon
- 1/2 red onion, thinly sliced
- Capers, for garnish
- Fresh dill, for garnish
- Lemon wedges, for serving

Instructions:

Prepare Bagels:
- Slice the bagels in half and toast them to your liking.

Spread Cream Cheese:
- Spread a generous layer of softened cream cheese on each half of the toasted bagels.

Layer Smoked Salmon:
- Arrange slices of smoked salmon evenly over the cream cheese on each bagel half.

Add Toppings:
- Top the smoked salmon with thinly sliced red onion. Sprinkle capers over the onions for a burst of briny flavor.

Garnish:
- Garnish the Smoked Salmon Bagels with fresh dill, adding a touch of herbaceous brightness.

Serve with Lemon Wedges:
- Serve the bagels with lemon wedges on the side. Squeezing a bit of lemon juice over the smoked salmon adds a refreshing zing.

Optional Extras:
- If desired, you can enhance the dish with additional toppings like sliced tomatoes, cucumber, or arugula.

Enjoy:
- Serve the Smoked Salmon Bagels immediately and enjoy this classic and delicious combination.

This Smoked Salmon Bagels with Cream Cheese recipe is a timeless favorite that showcases the rich, smoky flavor of Alaskan and Washingtonian smoked salmon. It's perfect for a leisurely breakfast, brunch, or a light and satisfying lunch. Enjoy the taste of the Pacific Northwest!

Idaho Huckleberry BBQ Sauce (Idaho)

Ingredients:

- 1 cup fresh or frozen Idaho huckleberries
- 1 cup ketchup
- 1/2 cup brown sugar, packed
- 1/4 cup apple cider vinegar
- 2 tablespoons Worcestershire sauce
- 1 tablespoon Dijon mustard
- 1 teaspoon garlic powder
- 1 teaspoon onion powder
- 1/2 teaspoon smoked paprika
- 1/2 teaspoon black pepper, freshly ground
- 1/4 teaspoon cayenne pepper (optional, for heat)
- Salt, to taste

Instructions:

Prepare Huckleberries:
- If using fresh huckleberries, rinse them thoroughly. If using frozen huckleberries, allow them to thaw.

Combine Ingredients:
- In a medium saucepan, combine the huckleberries, ketchup, brown sugar, apple cider vinegar, Worcestershire sauce, Dijon mustard, garlic powder, onion powder, smoked paprika, black pepper, and cayenne pepper if using.

Simmer:
- Bring the mixture to a gentle simmer over medium heat, stirring to combine the ingredients.

Cook Down:
- Reduce the heat to low and let the sauce simmer for 15-20 minutes, or until it thickens slightly. Stir occasionally to prevent sticking.

Adjust Seasoning:
- Taste the BBQ sauce and adjust the seasoning. Add salt to taste and more cayenne pepper if you want extra heat.

Blend (Optional):
- For a smoother consistency, you can use an immersion blender to blend the sauce until it reaches your desired smoothness.

Cool and Store:

- Allow the Idaho Huckleberry BBQ Sauce to cool before transferring it to a glass jar or airtight container. Store in the refrigerator.

Serve:
- Use the Idaho Huckleberry BBQ Sauce as a delicious condiment for grilled meats, burgers, or as a dipping sauce. Enjoy the unique and regional flavor of huckleberries in your barbecue experience!

This Idaho Huckleberry BBQ Sauce is a delightful blend of sweet, tart, and smoky flavors, making it a perfect accompaniment to various dishes. Whether you're grilling or dipping, this sauce will add a touch of Idaho's unique culinary charm to your meals.

Oregon Marionberry BBQ Chicken (Oregon)

Ingredients:

For the Marionberry BBQ Sauce:

- 1 cup fresh or frozen Oregon marionberries
- 1 cup ketchup
- 1/4 cup apple cider vinegar
- 1/4 cup honey
- 2 tablespoons molasses
- 2 tablespoons Dijon mustard
- 1 tablespoon Worcestershire sauce
- 1 teaspoon smoked paprika
- 1 teaspoon garlic powder
- 1/2 teaspoon onion powder
- Salt and black pepper, to taste

For the Grilled Chicken:

- 4 boneless, skinless chicken breasts
- Salt and black pepper, to season
- Olive oil, for brushing

Optional Garnish:

- Fresh marionberries for garnish
- Fresh cilantro, chopped, for garnish

Instructions:

Prepare Marionberry BBQ Sauce:

Combine Ingredients:
- In a saucepan, combine marionberries, ketchup, apple cider vinegar, honey, molasses, Dijon mustard, Worcestershire sauce, smoked paprika, garlic powder, onion powder, salt, and black pepper.

Simmer:

- Bring the mixture to a simmer over medium heat, stirring to combine the ingredients. Let it simmer for about 15-20 minutes, or until the marionberries break down, and the sauce thickens. Stir occasionally to prevent sticking.

Adjust Seasoning:
- Taste the BBQ sauce and adjust the seasoning to your liking. Add more salt, pepper, or honey if needed.

Blend (Optional):
- For a smoother consistency, you can use an immersion blender to blend the sauce until it reaches your desired texture.

Grill Chicken:

Preheat Grill:
- Preheat your grill to medium-high heat.

Season Chicken:
- Season the chicken breasts with salt and black pepper. Brush each side with olive oil.

Grill Chicken:
- Place the chicken breasts on the preheated grill. Grill for 6-8 minutes per side, or until the internal temperature reaches 165°F (74°C) and the chicken is cooked through.

Brush with Marionberry BBQ Sauce:
- In the last few minutes of grilling, brush the chicken breasts generously with the prepared marionberry BBQ sauce. Allow it to caramelize on the chicken.

Serve:

Garnish and Serve:
- Remove the grilled Marionberry BBQ Chicken from the grill. Garnish with fresh marionberries and chopped cilantro. Serve hot with additional BBQ sauce on the side.

This Oregon Marionberry BBQ Chicken is a perfect blend of savory, sweet, and tangy flavors. The marionberry BBQ sauce adds a unique touch to the grilled chicken, creating a delightful dish that showcases the local flavors of Oregon. Enjoy this delicious barbecue creation!

Montana Bison Burger with Wild Mushroom Sauce (Montana)

Ingredients:

For the Bison Burgers:

- 1 pound ground Montana bison meat
- Salt and black pepper, to taste
- 1 tablespoon olive oil
- 4 whole-grain or brioche burger buns

For the Wild Mushroom Sauce:

- 2 cups assorted wild mushrooms (such as chanterelles, morels, or shiitake), cleaned and sliced
- 2 tablespoons unsalted butter
- 2 cloves garlic, minced
- 1/4 cup dry red wine
- 1 cup beef or bison broth
- 2 tablespoons fresh thyme leaves
- Salt and black pepper, to taste

Optional Toppings:

- Swiss or Gruyère cheese, sliced
- Fresh arugula or spinach
- Caramelized onions

Instructions:

Prepare the Bison Burgers:

Season Bison Meat:
- In a bowl, season the ground bison meat with salt and black pepper. Gently mix to combine.

Form Patties:
- Divide the bison meat into four equal portions and shape them into burger patties.

Cook Burgers:

- Heat olive oil in a skillet or on a grill over medium-high heat. Cook the bison patties for about 4-5 minutes per side or until they reach your desired level of doneness.

Optional Cheese Topping:
- If using cheese, place a slice on each burger during the last minute of cooking to melt.

Toast Buns:
- Toast the burger buns on the grill or in a toaster until golden.

Prepare the Wild Mushroom Sauce:

Sauté Mushrooms:
- In a separate pan, melt butter over medium heat. Add sliced wild mushrooms and minced garlic. Sauté until the mushrooms are golden brown and the liquid has evaporated.

Deglaze with Wine:
- Pour in the red wine to deglaze the pan, scraping up any browned bits from the bottom.

Add Broth and Thyme:
- Stir in the beef or bison broth and fresh thyme leaves. Simmer for about 5-7 minutes, allowing the flavors to meld and the sauce to thicken slightly. Season with salt and black pepper to taste.

Assemble the Bison Burgers:

Build Burgers:
- Place each bison patty on a toasted bun. Top with a generous spoonful of the wild mushroom sauce.

Optional Toppings:
- Add additional toppings like Swiss or Gruyère cheese, fresh arugula or spinach, and caramelized onions if desired.

Serve:
- Serve the Montana Bison Burgers with Wild Mushroom Sauce immediately. Enjoy the robust flavors of bison and wild mushrooms in every bite!

This Montana Bison Burger with Wild Mushroom Sauce is a delightful combination of lean bison meat and the earthy richness of wild mushrooms. It's a taste of Montana's natural bounty in a delicious and hearty burger. Enjoy your culinary journey through Montana!

Northwestern Quinoa Salad (Regional)

Ingredients:

For the Salad:

- 1 cup quinoa, rinsed and cooked according to package instructions
- 1 cup cherry tomatoes, halved
- 1 cucumber, diced
- 1 red bell pepper, diced
- 1/2 cup red onion, finely chopped
- 1/2 cup feta cheese, crumbled
- 1/4 cup Kalamata olives, sliced
- 1/4 cup fresh parsley, chopped
- 1/4 cup fresh dill, chopped
- 1/4 cup roasted hazelnuts, chopped

For the Dressing:

- 1/4 cup extra-virgin olive oil
- 2 tablespoons red wine vinegar
- 1 tablespoon Dijon mustard
- 1 teaspoon honey
- Salt and black pepper, to taste

Instructions:

Prepare Quinoa:

Cook Quinoa:
- Rinse the quinoa under cold water. Cook it according to the package instructions. Once cooked, let it cool to room temperature.

Prepare the Salad:

Combine Ingredients:
- In a large bowl, combine the cooked quinoa, cherry tomatoes, cucumber, red bell pepper, red onion, feta cheese, Kalamata olives, fresh parsley, fresh dill, and roasted hazelnuts.

Prepare the Dressing:

- Whisk Dressing:
  - In a small bowl, whisk together the extra-virgin olive oil, red wine vinegar, Dijon mustard, honey, salt, and black pepper. Adjust the seasoning to your taste.

Assemble the Salad:

- Drizzle Dressing:
  - Drizzle the dressing over the salad ingredients.
- Toss Gently:
  - Gently toss the Northwestern Quinoa Salad until all ingredients are well coated with the dressing.

Chill and Serve:

- Chill (Optional):
  - For enhanced flavors, you can refrigerate the salad for about 30 minutes before serving.
- Serve:
  - Serve the Northwestern Quinoa Salad as a refreshing side dish or a light and nutritious main course. Garnish with additional herbs or hazelnuts if desired.

This Northwestern Quinoa Salad is a delightful medley of fresh vegetables, herbs, and the unique touch of hazelnuts, reflecting the culinary diversity of the Pacific Northwest. Enjoy the wholesome goodness of this vibrant and flavorful salad!

Alaska Halibut Tacos with Mango Salsa (Alaska)

Ingredients:

For the Halibut:

- 1 pound Alaska halibut fillets, skinless and boneless
- 2 tablespoons olive oil
- 1 teaspoon ground cumin
- 1 teaspoon chili powder
- Salt and black pepper, to taste
- Corn or flour tortillas

For the Mango Salsa:

- 1 ripe mango, peeled, pitted, and diced
- 1/2 red onion, finely chopped
- 1 red bell pepper, diced
- 1 jalapeño, seeded and finely chopped
- 1/4 cup fresh cilantro, chopped
- Juice of 1 lime
- Salt and black pepper, to taste

For the Cabbage Slaw:

- 2 cups shredded green cabbage
- 1 carrot, julienned
- 2 tablespoons mayonnaise
- 1 tablespoon apple cider vinegar
- Salt and black pepper, to taste

Optional Toppings:

- Avocado slices
- Fresh cilantro leaves
- Lime wedges

Instructions:

Prepare the Halibut:

Preheat Grill or Pan:
- Preheat a grill or grill pan over medium-high heat.

Season Halibut:
- In a small bowl, mix together olive oil, ground cumin, chili powder, salt, and black pepper. Brush the halibut fillets with this spice mixture.

Grill Halibut:
- Grill the halibut fillets for about 3-4 minutes per side, or until the fish is cooked through and flakes easily. Cooking time may vary based on thickness.

Flake Halibut:
- Once cooked, flake the halibut into bite-sized pieces.

Prepare the Mango Salsa:

Combine Ingredients:
- In a bowl, combine diced mango, chopped red onion, diced red bell pepper, jalapeño, cilantro, lime juice, salt, and black pepper. Mix well to create the mango salsa.

Prepare the Cabbage Slaw:

Combine Ingredients:
- In another bowl, mix shredded green cabbage, julienned carrot, mayonnaise, apple cider vinegar, salt, and black pepper to create the cabbage slaw.

Assemble the Tacos:

Warm Tortillas:
- Warm the tortillas in the grill or microwave until they are pliable.

Assemble Tacos:
- Spoon the flaked halibut onto each tortilla. Top with mango salsa and cabbage slaw.

Optional Toppings:
- Add optional toppings such as avocado slices, fresh cilantro leaves, and lime wedges.

Serve:

- Serve the Alaska Halibut Tacos with Mango Salsa immediately. Enjoy the delightful combination of fresh halibut, vibrant mango salsa, and crunchy cabbage slaw!

These Alaska Halibut Tacos with Mango Salsa offer a burst of flavors and textures in every bite, combining the best of Alaskan seafood with the tropical sweetness of mango. It's a perfect dish for a light and delicious meal!

Washington Apple and Gorgonzola Stuffed CHicken Breast (Washington)

Ingredients:

For the Stuffed Chicken:

- 4 boneless, skinless chicken breasts
- Salt and black pepper, to taste
- 1 tablespoon olive oil
- 1 large Washington apple, peeled, cored, and diced
- 1/2 cup Gorgonzola cheese, crumbled
- 2 tablespoons fresh sage, chopped

For the Apple Cider Glaze:

- 1 cup apple cider
- 2 tablespoons honey
- 1 tablespoon Dijon mustard
- 1 tablespoon balsamic vinegar
- Salt and black pepper, to taste

Instructions:

Prepare the Stuffed Chicken:

> Preheat Oven:
> - Preheat your oven to 375°F (190°C).
>
> Butterfly Chicken Breasts:
> - Lay each chicken breast flat on a cutting board. Carefully butterfly each breast by slicing horizontally, keeping the other side intact.
>
> Season and Stuff:
> - Season the inside of each butterflied chicken breast with salt and black pepper. Fill each breast with diced Washington apple, Gorgonzola cheese, and chopped sage.
>
> Fold and Secure:
> - Fold the chicken breasts over the stuffing and secure with toothpicks to hold the shape.
>
> Season Outside:
> - Season the outside of each stuffed chicken breast with additional salt and black pepper.
>
> Sear Chicken:

- In an oven-safe skillet, heat olive oil over medium-high heat. Sear the stuffed chicken breasts on each side until golden brown.

Prepare the Apple Cider Glaze:

   Combine Ingredients:
   - In a small bowl, whisk together apple cider, honey, Dijon mustard, balsamic vinegar, salt, and black pepper.

   Glaze Chicken:
   - Pour the apple cider glaze over the seared chicken breasts.

Finish in the Oven:

   Bake:
   - Transfer the skillet to the preheated oven and bake for 20-25 minutes or until the chicken is cooked through and reaches an internal temperature of 165°F (74°C).

   Baste:
   - Baste the chicken with the glaze from the pan halfway through the baking time.

Serve:

   Rest and Serve:
   - Remove the stuffed chicken breasts from the oven and let them rest for a few minutes. Remove toothpicks before serving.

   Slice and Plate:
   - Slice the stuffed chicken breasts into medallions and plate them. Drizzle with any remaining glaze from the pan.

Optional Garnish:

- Garnish with additional chopped sage for a burst of freshness.

This Washington Apple and Gorgonzola Stuffed Chicken Breast is a delightful combination of sweet and savory flavors, capturing the essence of Washington's apple orchards. Enjoy this dish with a side of roasted vegetables or a light salad for a delicious and elegant meal!

Oregon Pinot Noir Braised Short Ribs (Oregon)

Ingredients:

For the Short Ribs:

- 4 pounds beef short ribs
- Salt and black pepper, to taste
- 2 tablespoons vegetable oil
- 1 large onion, diced
- 2 carrots, diced
- 3 cloves garlic, minced
- 2 tablespoons tomato paste
- 1 bottle (750 ml) Oregon Pinot Noir wine
- 2 cups beef broth
- 2 sprigs fresh thyme
- 2 bay leaves

For the Braising Liquid Reduction:

- 1/2 cup honey
- 2 tablespoons Dijon mustard
- Salt and black pepper, to taste

For Serving:

- Mashed potatoes or polenta
- Fresh parsley, chopped, for garnish

Instructions:

Prepare the Short Ribs:

Preheat Oven:
- Preheat your oven to 325°F (163°C).

Season Short Ribs:
- Season the short ribs with salt and black pepper.

Sear Short Ribs:

- In a large oven-safe Dutch oven or heavy pot, heat vegetable oil over medium-high heat. Sear the short ribs on all sides until browned. Work in batches if necessary. Remove the ribs and set aside.

Sauté Vegetables:
- In the same pot, add diced onion and carrots. Sauté until softened. Add minced garlic and cook for an additional minute.

Add Tomato Paste:
- Stir in the tomato paste and cook for 2 minutes to enhance its flavor.

Deglaze with Wine:
- Pour in the Oregon Pinot Noir wine, scraping up any browned bits from the bottom of the pot.

Combine Ingredients:
- Return the seared short ribs to the pot. Add beef broth, thyme sprigs, and bay leaves. Bring to a simmer.

Braise in the Oven:
- Cover the pot and transfer it to the preheated oven. Braise for 2.5 to 3 hours or until the short ribs are tender and falling off the bone.

Prepare the Reduction:

Make Reduction:
- In a small bowl, whisk together honey and Dijon mustard. About 30 minutes before the short ribs are done, remove the pot from the oven. Spoon off excess fat and stir in the honey-Dijon mixture. Return to the oven to finish cooking.

Serve:

Plate Short Ribs:
- Remove the short ribs from the pot and set aside. Discard thyme sprigs and bay leaves.

Skim Excess Fat:
- Skim any excess fat from the braising liquid.

Reduce Liquid:
- Place the pot over medium heat on the stovetop. Simmer the liquid until it reduces and thickens into a flavorful sauce.

Plate and Garnish:
- Serve the short ribs over mashed potatoes or polenta. Spoon the reduced braising liquid over the top. Garnish with chopped fresh parsley.

Enjoy this Oregon Pinot Noir Braised Short Ribs dish, which beautifully captures the essence of the region's renowned wine. The slow-braising process ensures that the short ribs are succulent and flavorful, making it a perfect centerpiece for a special meal!

Idaho Trout with Lemon-Dill Sauce (Idaho)

Ingredients:

For the Trout:

- 4 Idaho trout fillets
- Salt and black pepper, to taste
- 2 tablespoons olive oil
- 1 lemon, sliced for garnish

For the Lemon-Dill Sauce:

- 1/2 cup Greek yogurt
- Zest of 1 lemon
- Juice of 1 lemon
- 2 tablespoons fresh dill, chopped
- 1 tablespoon Dijon mustard
- 1 clove garlic, minced
- Salt and black pepper, to taste

Instructions:

Prepare the Trout:

Preheat Oven:
- Preheat your oven to 400°F (200°C).

Season Trout:
- Pat the trout fillets dry with paper towels. Season both sides with salt and black pepper.

Sear Trout:
- In an oven-safe skillet, heat olive oil over medium-high heat. Sear the trout fillets, skin side down, for 2-3 minutes or until the skin is crispy and golden.

Flip and Transfer to Oven:
- Carefully flip the trout fillets and transfer the skillet to the preheated oven. Bake for an additional 5-7 minutes or until the trout is cooked through and flakes easily.

Lemon Garnish:
- While baking, you can add a few lemon slices to the skillet for extra flavor.

Prepare the Lemon-Dill Sauce:

Combine Ingredients:
- In a bowl, whisk together Greek yogurt, lemon zest, lemon juice, chopped dill, Dijon mustard, minced garlic, salt, and black pepper. Adjust the seasoning to your liking.

Serve:

Plate Trout:
- Remove the trout fillets from the oven and place them on serving plates.

Drizzle Sauce:
- Drizzle the lemon-dill sauce generously over each trout fillet.

Garnish:
- Garnish with additional fresh dill and lemon slices.

Serve:
- Serve the Idaho Trout with Lemon-Dill Sauce immediately. This dish pairs well with steamed vegetables, rice, or a light salad.

Enjoy this Idaho Trout with Lemon-Dill Sauce, a simple yet elegant dish that lets the freshness of the trout shine, complemented by the vibrant flavors of lemon and dill. It's a perfect option for a quick and delicious dinner!

Montana Huckleberry Pancakes (Montana)

Ingredients:

- 1 cup all-purpose flour
- 2 tablespoons sugar
- 1 teaspoon baking powder
- 1/2 teaspoon baking soda
- 1/4 teaspoon salt
- 1 cup buttermilk
- 1 large egg
- 2 tablespoons unsalted butter, melted
- 1 teaspoon vanilla extract
- 1/2 cup fresh or frozen Montana huckleberries
- Maple syrup, for serving

Instructions:

Preheat Griddle or Pan:
- Preheat a griddle or non-stick pan over medium heat.

Prepare Dry Ingredients:
- In a mixing bowl, whisk together the flour, sugar, baking powder, baking soda, and salt.

Mix Wet Ingredients:
- In another bowl, whisk together the buttermilk, egg, melted butter, and vanilla extract.

Combine Wet and Dry Ingredients:
- Pour the wet ingredients into the dry ingredients and gently mix until just combined. It's okay if there are a few lumps.

Fold in Huckleberries:
- Gently fold in the Montana huckleberries into the pancake batter.

Cook Pancakes:
- Grease the griddle or pan with a bit of butter or cooking spray. Pour 1/4 cup portions of batter onto the hot griddle for each pancake. Cook until bubbles form on the surface and the edges look set, then flip and cook the other side until golden brown.

Repeat:
- Repeat until all the batter is used, adjusting the heat if necessary.

Keep Warm:
- Keep the cooked pancakes warm in a low oven while you finish the batch.

Serve:
- Serve the Montana Huckleberry Pancakes warm, stacked, and drizzled with maple syrup.

Optional Toppings:
- You can add additional huckleberries on top or a dollop of whipped cream for extra indulgence.

Enjoy these Montana Huckleberry Pancakes as a delightful breakfast or brunch, savoring the unique and delicious taste of huckleberries, a true Montana gem!

Northwestern Quiche with Smoked Salmon and Asparagus (Regional)

Ingredients:

For the Quiche Filling:

- 1 cup smoked salmon, flaked
- 1 cup asparagus, trimmed and chopped
- 1/2 cup red onion, finely chopped
- 1 cup Gruyère or Swiss cheese, shredded
- 4 large eggs
- 1 cup half-and-half or whole milk
- Salt and black pepper, to taste
- 1 tablespoon fresh dill, chopped

For the Quiche Crust:

- 1 1/4 cups all-purpose flour
- 1/2 cup unsalted butter, cold and diced
- 1/4 teaspoon salt
- 2-3 tablespoons ice water

Instructions:

Prepare the Quiche Crust:

Combine Ingredients:
- In a food processor, combine the flour, cold diced butter, and salt. Pulse until the mixture resembles coarse crumbs.

Add Ice Water:
- Gradually add ice water, one tablespoon at a time, and pulse until the dough just comes together.

Form Dough:
- Turn the dough out onto a floured surface and gently knead it into a disc. Wrap in plastic wrap and refrigerate for at least 30 minutes.

Preheat Oven:
- Preheat your oven to 375°F (190°C).

Roll Out Dough:
- Roll out the chilled dough on a floured surface and line a greased 9-inch tart or quiche pan with the rolled-out dough. Trim any excess.

Blind Bake (Optional):

- For a crispier crust, you can blind bake the crust. Line the crust with parchment paper, fill with pie weights or dried beans, and bake for about 10 minutes. Remove the weights and parchment, then bake for an additional 5 minutes.

Prepare the Quiche Filling:

Whisk Eggs and Milk:
- In a bowl, whisk together the eggs and half-and-half or whole milk. Season with salt and black pepper.

Assemble Filling:
- Sprinkle smoked salmon, chopped asparagus, red onion, and shredded cheese evenly over the prepared crust.

Pour Egg Mixture:
- Pour the egg and milk mixture over the filling ingredients.

Add Fresh Dill:
- Sprinkle chopped fresh dill over the top.

Bake the Quiche:

Bake:
- Bake in the preheated oven for 30-35 minutes or until the quiche is set and the top is golden brown.

Cool:
- Allow the quiche to cool slightly before slicing.

Serve:
- Serve the Northwestern Quiche with Smoked Salmon and Asparagus warm or at room temperature.

Enjoy this Northwestern-inspired quiche that combines the smoky richness of salmon, the freshness of asparagus, and the creamy texture of eggs in a flaky crust—a perfect dish for brunch or a light dinner!

Washington Cherry Balsamic Glazed Pork Chops (Washington)

Ingredients:

For the Pork Chops:

- 4 bone-in pork chops
- Salt and black pepper, to taste
- 2 tablespoons olive oil

For the Cherry Balsamic Glaze:

- 1 cup fresh or frozen Washington cherries, pitted and halved
- 1/2 cup balsamic vinegar
- 1/4 cup cherry preserves or jam
- 2 tablespoons honey
- 2 cloves garlic, minced
- 1 teaspoon Dijon mustard
- Salt and black pepper, to taste

Optional Garnish:

- Fresh parsley, chopped

Instructions:

Prepare the Pork Chops:

Preheat Oven:
- Preheat your oven to 375°F (190°C).

Season Pork Chops:
- Season the pork chops with salt and black pepper.

Sear Pork Chops:
- In an oven-safe skillet, heat olive oil over medium-high heat. Sear the pork chops on both sides until golden brown. This step is to develop flavor; the chops will finish cooking in the oven.

Bake:
- Transfer the skillet to the preheated oven and bake for about 15-20 minutes or until the internal temperature reaches 145°F (63°C) for medium doneness.

Prepare the Cherry Balsamic Glaze:

Simmer Ingredients:
- In a saucepan, combine Washington cherries, balsamic vinegar, cherry preserves or jam, honey, minced garlic, Dijon mustard, salt, and black pepper.

Simmer and Reduce:
- Bring the mixture to a simmer over medium heat. Reduce the heat and let it simmer for about 10-15 minutes, or until the cherries are softened, and the sauce has thickened slightly.

Adjust Seasoning:
- Taste the glaze and adjust the seasoning or sweetness according to your preference.

Finish and Serve:

Glaze Pork Chops:
- Once the pork chops are done baking, brush them with the cherry balsamic glaze during the last few minutes of cooking.

Serve:
- Plate the pork chops, drizzle with additional glaze, and garnish with chopped fresh parsley.

Optional Side:
- Serve the Washington Cherry Balsamic Glazed Pork Chops with your favorite side dishes, such as roasted vegetables or mashed potatoes.

Enjoy these succulent pork chops glazed with a sweet and tangy Washington cherry balsamic sauce. The combination of savory pork with the fruity glaze creates a delightful and flavorful dish, perfect for a special dinner!

Alaska King Crab Linguine (Alaska)

Ingredients:

- 1 pound Alaska king crab legs, cooked and meat removed from the shell
- 12 ounces linguine or your favorite pasta
- 2 tablespoons unsalted butter
- 2 tablespoons olive oil
- 4 cloves garlic, minced
- 1/2 teaspoon red pepper flakes (adjust to taste)
- 1/2 cup dry white wine
- 1 cup cherry tomatoes, halved
- 1/4 cup fresh parsley, chopped
- Zest of 1 lemon
- Juice of 1 lemon
- Salt and black pepper, to taste
- Grated Parmesan cheese, for serving

Instructions:

Prepare Crab Meat:
- If the Alaska king crab legs are not already cooked, steam or boil them until the meat is opaque and flakes easily. Remove the crab meat from the shells and set aside.

Cook Linguine:
- Cook the linguine according to the package instructions until al dente. Drain and set aside.

Sauté Garlic and Red Pepper Flakes:
- In a large skillet, heat the butter and olive oil over medium heat. Add minced garlic and red pepper flakes. Sauté for 1-2 minutes until the garlic becomes fragrant.

Add Crab Meat:
- Add the Alaska king crab meat to the skillet and toss to coat in the garlic and red pepper mixture. Cook for 2-3 minutes to heat the crab through.

Deglaze with White Wine:
- Pour in the dry white wine to deglaze the skillet, scraping up any browned bits from the bottom.

Add Cherry Tomatoes:
- Add halved cherry tomatoes to the skillet. Cook for an additional 2-3 minutes until the tomatoes soften.

Combine with Linguine:
- Add the cooked linguine to the skillet, tossing to combine with the crab and tomato mixture.

Add Lemon Zest and Juice:
- Stir in the lemon zest and lemon juice. Toss everything together until well combined.

Season and Garnish:
- Season the Alaska King Crab Linguine with salt and black pepper to taste. Stir in chopped fresh parsley for added freshness.

Serve:
- Divide the linguine and crab mixture among plates. Garnish with grated Parmesan cheese.

Enjoy this Alaska King Crab Linguine, where the sweet and delicate flavor of the king crab complements the pasta perfectly. It's a delightful dish that captures the essence of Alaska's seafood bounty!

Idaho Potato Gnocchi with Sage Butter (Idaho)

Ingredients:

For the Potato Gnocchi:

- 2 large Idaho potatoes, baked or boiled until tender
- 1 egg, lightly beaten
- 1 1/2 cups all-purpose flour, plus extra for dusting
- Salt, to taste

For the Sage Butter Sauce:

- 1/2 cup unsalted butter
- Fresh sage leaves
- Salt and black pepper, to taste
- Grated Parmesan cheese, for serving (optional)

Instructions:

Prepare the Potato Gnocchi:

Prepare Potatoes:
- Bake or boil the Idaho potatoes until they are fork-tender. Let them cool slightly.

Peel and Mash:
- Peel the potatoes and mash them while they are still warm, ensuring a smooth consistency.

Add Egg and Flour:
- In a large bowl, combine the mashed potatoes with the beaten egg. Gradually add the flour and a pinch of salt, mixing until the dough comes together.

Knead Gently:
- Turn the dough out onto a lightly floured surface and knead gently. Be cautious not to over-knead; you want the dough to be soft and slightly sticky.

Divide and Roll:
- Divide the dough into small portions. Roll each portion into a long, thin rope, about 1/2 inch in diameter.

Cut into Gnocchi:
- Cut the ropes into bite-sized pieces to form the gnocchi. Optionally, you can use a fork to create ridges on the gnocchi.

Boil Gnocchi:

- Bring a large pot of salted water to a boil. Drop the gnocchi into the boiling water and cook until they float to the surface. Remove with a slotted spoon and set aside.

Prepare the Sage Butter Sauce:

Sauté Sage Leaves:
- In a skillet, melt the butter over medium heat. Add fresh sage leaves and let them sizzle for a minute or two until they become fragrant and slightly crispy.

Add Gnocchi:
- Gently add the boiled gnocchi to the sage-infused butter. Toss until the gnocchi are well-coated in the buttery sauce.

Season and Serve:
- Season with salt and black pepper to taste. Optionally, sprinkle with grated Parmesan cheese.

Plate and Garnish:
- Plate the Idaho Potato Gnocchi with Sage Butter and garnish with additional fresh sage leaves and Parmesan, if desired.

Serve Warm:
- Serve the gnocchi immediately, savoring the comforting combination of pillowy potato dumplings and fragrant sage butter.

Enjoy this Idaho Potato Gnocchi with Sage Butter as a comforting and flavorful dish that perfectly captures the essence of Idaho's iconic potatoes!

Northwestern Berry Cobbler (Regional)

Ingredients:

For the Berry Filling:

- 4 cups mixed berries (such as blackberries, raspberries, blueberries, and huckleberries)
- 1/2 cup granulated sugar
- 2 tablespoons cornstarch
- 1 tablespoon lemon juice
- Zest of 1 lemon

For the Cobbler Topping:

- 1 cup all-purpose flour
- 1/2 cup granulated sugar
- 1 teaspoon baking powder
- 1/4 teaspoon salt
- 1/2 cup unsalted butter, cold and cut into small cubes
- 1/3 cup boiling water

For Serving:

- Vanilla ice cream or whipped cream (optional)

Instructions:

Prepare the Berry Filling:

> Preheat Oven:
> - Preheat your oven to 375°F (190°C).
>
> Combine Ingredients:
> - In a large mixing bowl, gently toss together the mixed berries, granulated sugar, cornstarch, lemon juice, and lemon zest until the berries are well coated.
>
> Transfer to Baking Dish:
> - Transfer the berry mixture to a greased 9x13-inch baking dish or a similar-sized casserole dish.

Prepare the Cobbler Topping:

Mix Dry Ingredients:
- In another bowl, whisk together the flour, sugar, baking powder, and salt.

Cut in Butter:
- Add the cold, cubed butter to the dry ingredients. Use a pastry cutter or your fingers to cut the butter into the flour mixture until it resembles coarse crumbs.

Add Boiling Water:
- Pour the boiling water over the flour and butter mixture. Stir until just combined.

Assemble and Bake:

Drop Topping Over Berries:
- Drop spoonfuls of the cobbler topping evenly over the berry mixture.

Bake:
- Bake in the preheated oven for 35-40 minutes or until the topping is golden brown, and the berries are bubbling.

Cool Slightly:
- Allow the cobbler to cool slightly before serving.

Serve:

Serve Warm:
- Serve the Northwestern Berry Cobbler warm, either on its own or with a scoop of vanilla ice cream or a dollop of whipped cream.

Enjoy:
- Enjoy the delightful combination of sweet, juicy berries and the buttery, tender cobbler topping!

This Northwestern Berry Cobbler is a perfect way to showcase the abundance of berries in the region. It's a comforting and flavorful dessert that's sure to be a hit!

Oregon Hazelnut-Crusted Tilapia (Oregon)

Ingredients:

For the Hazelnut Crust:

- 1 cup Oregon hazelnuts, finely chopped
- 1/2 cup breadcrumbs
- 1/4 cup grated Parmesan cheese
- 1 teaspoon dried oregano
- Salt and black pepper, to taste

For the Tilapia:

- 4 tilapia fillets
- 1/2 cup all-purpose flour
- 2 large eggs, beaten
- Olive oil, for frying

For the Lemon-Herb Butter Sauce:

- 1/2 cup unsalted butter
- Zest and juice of 1 lemon
- 2 tablespoons fresh parsley, chopped
- Salt and black pepper, to taste

Instructions:

Prepare the Hazelnut Crust:

Combine Ingredients:
- In a shallow bowl, combine finely chopped Oregon hazelnuts, breadcrumbs, grated Parmesan cheese, dried oregano, salt, and black pepper. Mix well.

Prepare the Tilapia:

Coat Tilapia:
- Pat the tilapia fillets dry with paper towels. Dredge each fillet in all-purpose flour, then dip into the beaten eggs, and finally, coat with the hazelnut crust mixture, pressing the crust onto the fillets to adhere.

Set Aside:
- Place the hazelnut-crusted tilapia fillets on a plate and let them rest for a few minutes to allow the crust to set.

Cook the Tilapia:

Heat Olive Oil:
- In a large skillet, heat olive oil over medium-high heat.

Pan-Fry Tilapia:
- Pan-fry the hazelnut-crusted tilapia fillets for about 3-4 minutes per side or until the crust is golden brown, and the fish is cooked through. Cooking time may vary depending on the thickness of the fillets.

Transfer to Plate:
- Once cooked, transfer the tilapia fillets to a serving plate.

Prepare the Lemon-Herb Butter Sauce:

Melt Butter:
- In the same skillet, melt the unsalted butter over medium heat.

Add Lemon Zest and Juice:
- Add the lemon zest and juice to the melted butter, stirring to combine.

Season and Garnish:
- Season the sauce with salt and black pepper to taste. Stir in the chopped fresh parsley.

Serve:

Pour Sauce Over Tilapia:
- Pour the lemon-herb butter sauce over the hazelnut-crusted tilapia fillets.

Garnish and Enjoy:
- Garnish with additional chopped hazelnuts and parsley if desired. Serve the Oregon Hazelnut-Crusted Tilapia immediately, and enjoy the delightful flavors!

This Oregon-inspired dish offers a perfect blend of Oregon hazelnuts and tilapia, creating a crunchy and flavorful crust with a zesty lemon-herb butter sauce. Enjoy this delightful and nutty seafood dish!

Washington Potato Leek Soup (Washington)

Ingredients:

- 4 large russet potatoes, peeled and diced
- 3 leeks, cleaned and sliced (white and light green parts only)
- 1 onion, finely chopped
- 3 cloves garlic, minced
- 4 cups vegetable or chicken broth
- 1 cup whole milk or heavy cream
- 2 tablespoons unsalted butter
- 2 tablespoons olive oil
- Salt and black pepper, to taste
- Chives or green onions, chopped (for garnish)
- Grated cheddar cheese (optional, for garnish)

Instructions:

Prepare Vegetables:
- Peel and dice the russet potatoes, clean and slice the leeks (white and light green parts only), and finely chop the onion and garlic.

Sauté Aromatics:
- In a large pot, heat the butter and olive oil over medium heat. Add the chopped onion and leeks, sautéing until they become soft and translucent, about 5-7 minutes.

Add Garlic:
- Add minced garlic to the pot and sauté for an additional 1-2 minutes until fragrant.

Add Potatoes:
- Stir in the diced potatoes, coating them with the sautéed leek and onion mixture.

Pour in Broth:
- Pour in the vegetable or chicken broth, ensuring the potatoes are fully submerged. Bring the mixture to a simmer.

Simmer Until Potatoes are Tender:
- Reduce the heat to low and let the soup simmer for about 15-20 minutes or until the potatoes are tender when pierced with a fork.

Blend Soup:
- Use an immersion blender to carefully blend the soup until smooth. Alternatively, transfer the soup in batches to a blender, blending until smooth, and then return it to the pot.

Add Milk or Cream:

- Pour in the whole milk or heavy cream, stirring to combine. Allow the soup to simmer for an additional 5 minutes, ensuring it's heated through.

Season:
- Season the soup with salt and black pepper to taste. Adjust the seasoning as needed.

Serve:
- Ladle the Washington Potato Leek Soup into bowls. Garnish with chopped chives or green onions and, if desired, a sprinkle of grated cheddar cheese.

Enjoy:
- Serve the soup hot, savoring the comforting flavors of Washington-grown potatoes and leeks.

This Washington Potato Leek Soup is not only delicious but also captures the essence of locally sourced ingredients, making it a perfect choice for a warm and comforting meal. Enjoy!

Idaho Sun-Dried Tomato and Basil Stuffed Chicken (Idaho)

Ingredients:

For the Chicken:

- 4 boneless, skinless chicken breasts
- Salt and black pepper, to taste
- 1 tablespoon olive oil

For the Stuffing:

- 1/2 cup sun-dried tomatoes, finely chopped
- 1/4 cup fresh basil leaves, chopped
- 1/2 cup mozzarella cheese, shredded
- 1/4 cup Parmesan cheese, grated
- 2 cloves garlic, minced
- 1 tablespoon olive oil
- Salt and black pepper, to taste

For the Pan Sauce:

- 1/2 cup chicken broth
- 1/4 cup white wine (optional)
- 2 tablespoons unsalted butter
- Salt and black pepper, to taste

Instructions:

Prepare the Stuffing:

Rehydrate Sun-Dried Tomatoes:
- If using dried sun-dried tomatoes, rehydrate them by soaking in hot water for about 15 minutes. Drain and chop finely.

Prepare Stuffing Mixture:
- In a bowl, combine the chopped sun-dried tomatoes, fresh basil, mozzarella cheese, Parmesan cheese, minced garlic, olive oil, salt, and black pepper. Mix well.

Prepare the Chicken:

Preheat Oven:
- Preheat your oven to 375°F (190°C).

Butterfly Chicken Breasts:
- Lay each chicken breast flat on a cutting board. Carefully butterfly each chicken breast by making a horizontal cut through the center, stopping about 1/2 inch from the edge, creating a pocket.

Season Chicken:
- Season the inside of each chicken breast with salt and black pepper.

Stuff Chicken:
- Stuff each chicken breast with the sun-dried tomato and basil mixture, dividing it evenly among the breasts. Secure with toothpicks if needed.

Sear Chicken:
- In an oven-safe skillet, heat olive oil over medium-high heat. Sear the stuffed chicken breasts on both sides until golden brown, about 2-3 minutes per side.

Finish in Oven:
- Transfer the skillet to the preheated oven and bake for about 20-25 minutes or until the chicken is cooked through.

Prepare the Pan Sauce:

Deglaze Pan:
- In the same skillet, deglaze with chicken broth and white wine (if using), scraping up any browned bits from the bottom of the pan.

Add Butter:
- Stir in butter until melted. Season the pan sauce with salt and black pepper to taste.

Serve:

Slice and Plate:
- Slice the stuffed chicken breasts and plate them. Drizzle the pan sauce over the top.

Garnish:
- Garnish with additional fresh basil leaves, if desired.

Enjoy:
- Serve the Idaho Sun-Dried Tomato and Basil Stuffed Chicken hot, savoring the delicious combination of flavors.

This Idaho-inspired dish is a flavorful and elegant way to showcase sun-dried tomatoes and fresh basil while enjoying a succulent stuffed chicken breast. Enjoy your meal!

Montana Bison and Barley Soup (Montana)

Ingredients:

- 1 pound ground Montana bison
- 1 cup barley, rinsed
- 1 large onion, diced
- 3 carrots, peeled and sliced
- 3 celery stalks, sliced
- 4 cloves garlic, minced
- 8 cups beef or bison broth
- 1 can (14 oz) diced tomatoes
- 2 bay leaves
- 1 teaspoon dried thyme
- Salt and black pepper, to taste
- 2 tablespoons olive oil
- Fresh parsley, chopped (for garnish)

Instructions:

Sauté Bison:
- In a large soup pot, heat olive oil over medium heat. Add the ground Montana bison and cook until browned, breaking it apart with a spoon. Remove any excess fat.

Add Vegetables:
- Add diced onion, sliced carrots, sliced celery, and minced garlic to the pot. Sauté for about 5 minutes until the vegetables are softened.

Add Barley:
- Stir in the rinsed barley and cook for an additional 2 minutes, allowing the barley to toast slightly.

Pour in Broth:
- Pour in the beef or bison broth, diced tomatoes (with their juices), bay leaves, and dried thyme. Bring the mixture to a boil.

Simmer:
- Reduce the heat to low, cover the pot, and let the soup simmer for about 40-45 minutes or until the barley is tender.

Season:
- Season the soup with salt and black pepper to taste. Adjust the seasoning as needed.

Finish and Garnish:
- Once the barley is cooked, remove the bay leaves. Taste and adjust the seasoning if necessary. Stir in fresh parsley for added freshness.

Serve:
- Ladle the Montana Bison and Barley Soup into bowls and serve hot.

Enjoy:
- Enjoy the hearty and wholesome flavors of this Montana-inspired soup!

This Bison and Barley Soup is not only delicious but also a great way to showcase the unique taste of Montana bison. The combination of lean bison, hearty barley, and flavorful vegetables creates a comforting and satisfying meal.

Alaska Smoked Salmon and Avocado Salad (Alaska)

Ingredients:

For the Salad:

- 8 oz Alaska smoked salmon, flaked
- 2 ripe avocados, diced
- 1 cup cherry tomatoes, halved
- 1 cucumber, diced
- 1/4 red onion, thinly sliced
- 1/4 cup capers, drained
- Fresh dill, chopped (for garnish)

For the Dressing:

- 3 tablespoons extra-virgin olive oil
- 1 tablespoon Dijon mustard
- 2 tablespoons fresh lemon juice
- 1 clove garlic, minced
- Salt and black pepper, to taste

Instructions:

Prepare the Salad:

Flake Smoked Salmon:
- Carefully flake the Alaska smoked salmon into bite-sized pieces, removing any skin or bones.

Combine Ingredients:
- In a large salad bowl, combine the flaked smoked salmon, diced avocados, cherry tomatoes, diced cucumber, sliced red onion, and capers.

Prepare the Dressing:

Whisk Dressing:
- In a small bowl, whisk together the extra-virgin olive oil, Dijon mustard, fresh lemon juice, minced garlic, salt, and black pepper until well combined.

Assemble the Salad:

Drizzle Dressing:
- Drizzle the dressing over the smoked salmon and vegetable mixture.

Gently Toss:
- Gently toss the salad to coat the ingredients evenly with the dressing.

Garnish and Serve:

Garnish with Fresh Dill:
- Sprinkle fresh chopped dill over the salad for a burst of herbaceous flavor.

Serve Chilled:
- Refrigerate the Alaska Smoked Salmon and Avocado Salad for at least 30 minutes to allow the flavors to meld.

Serve:
- Serve the salad chilled, either as a refreshing appetizer or a light main dish.

Enjoy:
- Enjoy the vibrant and delicious flavors of Alaska with this Smoked Salmon and Avocado Salad!

This salad is not only a celebration of Alaska's smoked salmon but also a refreshing and nutritious dish that's perfect for a light lunch or as an appetizer. Enjoy!

Northwestern Wild Mushroom and Spinach Frittata (Regional)

Ingredients:

- 8 large eggs
- 1 cup wild mushrooms, cleaned and sliced (such as chanterelles or morel mushrooms)
- 2 cups fresh spinach, washed and chopped
- 1/2 cup shredded Gruyere cheese
- 1/4 cup grated Parmesan cheese
- 1/2 onion, finely chopped
- 2 cloves garlic, minced
- 2 tablespoons olive oil
- Salt and black pepper, to taste
- 1 tablespoon fresh thyme leaves
- 1 tablespoon butter (for greasing the pan)

Instructions:

Preheat Oven:
- Preheat your oven's broiler.

Sauté Mushrooms and Spinach:
- In an oven-safe skillet, heat olive oil over medium heat. Add chopped onions and sauté until softened. Add sliced wild mushrooms and cook until they release their moisture. Add minced garlic and cook for an additional minute. Stir in fresh spinach and cook until wilted. Season with salt and black pepper to taste.

Whisk Eggs:
- In a bowl, whisk the eggs until well beaten. Season with a pinch of salt and black pepper.

Add Eggs to Skillet:
- Pour the beaten eggs evenly over the sautéed mushrooms, spinach, and onions in the skillet. Allow the eggs to set around the edges.

Add Cheeses and Thyme:
- Sprinkle shredded Gruyere and grated Parmesan cheeses evenly over the eggs. Add fresh thyme leaves for added flavor.

Broil Frittata:
- Transfer the skillet to the preheated oven's broiler and broil for 3-5 minutes, or until the frittata is set in the center and the top is lightly golden.

Finish Under Broiler:
- Keep a close eye on the frittata as it finishes under the broiler to avoid overcooking.

Remove and Serve:
- Once the Northwestern Wild Mushroom and Spinach Frittata is cooked through and golden on top, remove it from the oven.

Let it Rest:
- Allow the frittata to rest for a couple of minutes before slicing.

Slice and Garnish:
- Slice the frittata into wedges and serve warm. Garnish with additional fresh thyme if desired.

Enjoy:
- Enjoy the savory goodness of this Northwestern-inspired frittata with wild mushrooms, spinach, and a blend of cheeses!

This frittata is not only a delicious breakfast or brunch option but also a fantastic way to showcase the flavors of the Northwestern region. Enjoy!

Washington Apple and Cheddar Grilled Cheese (Washington)

Ingredients:

- 8 slices of your favorite bread (sourdough or whole wheat work well)
- 2 Washington apples, thinly sliced (such as Honeycrisp or Fuji)
- 8 slices sharp cheddar cheese
- Butter, softened
- Dijon mustard (optional)
- Honey (optional, for drizzling)
- Fresh thyme leaves (optional, for garnish)

Instructions:

Preheat Griddle or Skillet:
- Preheat a griddle or non-stick skillet over medium heat.

Butter Bread Slices:
- Spread a thin layer of softened butter on one side of each slice of bread.

Assemble Sandwiches:
- On the non-buttered side of half the slices, place a slice of cheddar cheese, a layer of thinly sliced Washington apples, and another slice of cheddar cheese. If desired, add a thin layer of Dijon mustard on the other half of the slices.

Create Sandwiches:
- Place the remaining slices of bread on top, buttered side facing out, to create sandwiches.

Grill Sandwiches:
- Carefully place the sandwiches on the preheated griddle or skillet. Grill until the bread turns golden brown and the cheese starts to melt, about 3-4 minutes per side.

Press if Desired:
- If you prefer a flatter sandwich, you can press it down with a spatula while grilling.

Drizzle with Honey (Optional):
- If desired, drizzle a bit of honey over the apple slices before closing the sandwich for an extra touch of sweetness.

Garnish with Thyme (Optional):
- Garnish the sandwiches with fresh thyme leaves for a burst of herbaceous flavor.

Serve Warm:

- Once the Washington Apple and Cheddar Grilled Cheese sandwiches are golden brown and the cheese is melted, remove them from the griddle or skillet.

Slice and Enjoy:
- Slice the sandwiches in half and serve them warm. Enjoy the delicious combination of sweet Washington apples and melted cheddar cheese!

This grilled cheese is a delightful way to celebrate the flavors of Washington. The combination of sweet apples, sharp cheddar, and optional honey creates a perfectly balanced and comforting sandwich. Enjoy!

Idaho Potato and Chorizo Breakfast Burritos (Idaho)

Ingredients:

For the Potato and Chorizo Filling:

- 1 lb Idaho potatoes, peeled and diced into small cubes
- 1/2 lb chorizo sausage, casing removed
- 1 onion, finely chopped
- 2 cloves garlic, minced
- Salt and black pepper, to taste
- 1 teaspoon ground cumin
- 1 teaspoon smoked paprika
- 1/2 cup fresh cilantro, chopped

For the Burritos:

- Large flour tortillas
- Eggs (scrambled or fried, depending on preference)
- Shredded cheese (cheddar, Monterey Jack, or your choice)
- Salsa or hot sauce (optional)
- Avocado slices (optional)
- Sour cream (optional)

Instructions:

Prepare the Potato and Chorizo Filling:

Cook Potatoes:
- Boil or steam the diced Idaho potatoes until they are fork-tender. Drain and set aside.

Cook Chorizo:
- In a large skillet, cook the chorizo over medium heat, breaking it apart with a spoon as it cooks.

Add Aromatics:
- Once the chorizo starts to brown, add finely chopped onions and minced garlic. Cook until the onions are soft and translucent.

Add Potatoes and Spices:
- Add the cooked Idaho potatoes to the skillet. Season with salt, black pepper, ground cumin, and smoked paprika. Mix well and cook for a few more minutes until everything is well combined.

Finish with Cilantro:
- Stir in fresh cilantro, and let the mixture cook for an additional minute. Remove from heat.

Assemble the Burritos:

Warm Tortillas:
- Warm the flour tortillas in a dry skillet or microwave.

Layer Ingredients:
- On each tortilla, add a portion of the potato and chorizo filling, scrambled or fried eggs, shredded cheese, and any optional toppings like salsa, hot sauce, avocado slices, or sour cream.

Fold and Roll:
- Fold in the sides of the tortilla and then roll it up tightly to form a burrito.

Serve Warm:
- Place the burritos seam side down on a serving plate. Serve immediately, and enjoy your Idaho Potato and Chorizo Breakfast Burritos!

This breakfast burrito combines the hearty texture of Idaho potatoes with the flavorful kick of chorizo, creating a satisfying and delicious morning meal. Customize the toppings to your liking for a truly delightful breakfast experience!

Oregon Marionberry Sorbet (Oregon)

Ingredients:

- 4 cups fresh or frozen Oregon marionberries
- 1 cup granulated sugar
- 1 cup water
- 2 tablespoons fresh lemon juice
- 1 teaspoon lemon zest

Instructions:

Prepare Marionberries:
- If using fresh marionberries, wash them thoroughly. If using frozen marionberries, let them thaw slightly.

Make Simple Syrup:
- In a saucepan, combine sugar and water. Heat over medium heat, stirring until the sugar completely dissolves. Allow the simple syrup to cool.

Blend Marionberries:
- In a blender or food processor, puree the marionberries until smooth.

Strain (Optional):
- If you prefer a smoother sorbet, you can strain the marionberry puree through a fine-mesh sieve to remove seeds. This step is optional, as some people enjoy the texture of the seeds.

Combine Ingredients:
- In a bowl, mix the marionberry puree with the cooled simple syrup. Add fresh lemon juice and lemon zest. Stir until well combined.

Chill Mixture:
- Cover the bowl and refrigerate the mixture for at least 2-3 hours or until it's thoroughly chilled.

Churn Sorbet:
- Pour the chilled marionberry mixture into an ice cream maker and churn according to the manufacturer's instructions.

Transfer to Container:
- Once the sorbet reaches a soft-serve consistency, transfer it to a lidded container.

Freeze:
- Freeze the marionberry sorbet for an additional 4-6 hours or until firm.

Serve:

- Scoop the Oregon Marionberry Sorbet into bowls or cones. Garnish with fresh marionberries or a sprig of mint if desired.

Enjoy:
- Enjoy the cool and fruity taste of this homemade Oregon Marionberry Sorbet, perfect for a refreshing treat on a warm day!

This sorbet captures the essence of Oregon's famous marionberries, offering a delightful and natural sweetness. Feel free to adjust the sugar and lemon juice quantities based on your taste preferences. Enjoy!

Northwestern Lox and Bagel Brunch Board (Regional)

Ingredients:

For the Board:

- Assorted bagels (plain, everything, or your favorites)
- Smoked salmon (lox), thinly sliced
- Cream cheese (plain and flavored varieties)
- Red onion, thinly sliced
- Capers
- Fresh dill, chopped
- Lemon wedges

Optional Accompaniments:

- Sliced tomatoes
- Cucumber slices
- Radishes, thinly sliced
- Avocado slices
- Hard-boiled eggs, sliced
- Mixed olives
- Pickled red onions
- Sprouts (such as alfalfa or broccoli sprouts)

Instructions:

Prepare Bagels:
- Slice the bagels into halves or quarters, depending on their size.

Arrange Lox:
- Lay out the thinly sliced smoked salmon (lox) on a serving platter or board.

Set Up Cream Cheese Station:
- Place different varieties of cream cheese in small bowls or on the board. Consider plain cream cheese as well as flavored options like chive, garlic, or dill.

Add Fresh Ingredients:
- Arrange fresh red onion slices, capers, and chopped fresh dill on the board. These ingredients complement the lox and cream cheese.

Provide Lemon Wedges:
- Include lemon wedges on the board for guests to squeeze over their bagels or salmon.

Include Optional Accompaniments:

- Arrange additional accompaniments like sliced tomatoes, cucumber slices, radishes, avocado slices, hard-boiled eggs, mixed olives, pickled red onions, and sprouts on the board.

Create Sections:
- Consider creating sections on the board for different elements, making it visually appealing and easy for guests to navigate.

Garnish:
- Garnish the board with extra dill sprigs or other fresh herbs for an added touch.

Serve with Beverages:
- Offer beverages like coffee, tea, or fresh orange juice to complement the brunch spread.

Enjoy:
- Invite guests to create their own bagel sandwiches with the lox, cream cheese, and various toppings. It's a customizable and delightful brunch experience.

This Northwestern Lox and Bagel Brunch Board brings together the classic flavors of lox and bagels with a variety of accompaniments, offering a perfect balance of savory and fresh elements. Enjoy your brunch!

Alaska Halibut Chowder (Alaska)

Ingredients:

- 1 lb Alaska halibut fillets, skin removed, cut into bite-sized pieces
- 3 slices bacon, diced
- 1 onion, finely chopped
- 2 celery stalks, diced
- 2 carrots, diced
- 2 cloves garlic, minced
- 3 cups potatoes, peeled and diced
- 4 cups chicken or vegetable broth
- 1 bay leaf
- 1 teaspoon dried thyme
- 1/2 teaspoon dried dill
- Salt and black pepper, to taste
- 1 cup frozen corn kernels
- 2 cups whole milk
- 1 cup heavy cream
- 3 tablespoons all-purpose flour
- Fresh parsley, chopped (for garnish)

Instructions:

Cook Bacon:
- In a large pot, cook diced bacon over medium heat until it becomes crispy. Remove excess grease, leaving about 1 tablespoon in the pot.

Sauté Vegetables:
- Add chopped onion, celery, carrots, and minced garlic to the pot. Sauté until the vegetables are softened.

Add Potatoes and Broth:
- Stir in diced potatoes, chicken or vegetable broth, bay leaf, dried thyme, dried dill, salt, and black pepper. Bring the mixture to a simmer and cook until the potatoes are tender.

Prepare Halibut:
- In a separate pan, lightly cook the halibut pieces until they are just opaque. Be careful not to overcook, as the halibut will continue to cook in the chowder.

Add Corn:
- Add frozen corn kernels to the pot and continue to simmer for a few more minutes.

Create Roux:

- In a small bowl, whisk together flour and a small amount of milk to create a smooth paste (roux).

Add Milk and Cream:
- Pour the remaining milk and heavy cream into the pot. Gradually whisk in the roux, stirring continuously to avoid lumps. Cook until the chowder thickens.

Incorporate Halibut:
- Gently fold in the cooked halibut pieces, allowing them to heat through.

Adjust Seasoning:
- Taste the chowder and adjust the seasoning with salt and black pepper as needed.

Serve:
- Ladle the Alaska Halibut Chowder into bowls. Garnish with chopped fresh parsley.

Enjoy:
- Enjoy this hearty and flavorful Alaska Halibut Chowder, celebrating the rich taste of halibut in a comforting soup!

This chowder is a delightful way to showcase the delicious and mild flavor of Alaska halibut, making it a perfect dish for colder days. Serve it with crusty bread for a complete and satisfying meal!

Washington Apple Walnut Salad (Washington)

Ingredients:

For the Salad:

- 4 cups mixed salad greens (spinach, arugula, or your choice)
- 2 Washington apples, cored and thinly sliced
- 1 cup red grapes, halved
- 1/2 cup crumbled feta cheese
- 1/2 cup chopped walnuts, toasted
- 1/4 red onion, thinly sliced

For the Dressing:

- 3 tablespoons extra-virgin olive oil
- 2 tablespoons apple cider vinegar
- 1 tablespoon honey
- 1 teaspoon Dijon mustard
- Salt and black pepper, to taste

Instructions:

Prepare the Salad:

Toast Walnuts:
- In a dry skillet over medium heat, toast the chopped walnuts until they become fragrant. Be careful not to burn them. Set aside to cool.

Assemble Salad:
- In a large salad bowl, combine the mixed salad greens, thinly sliced Washington apples, halved red grapes, crumbled feta cheese, toasted walnuts, and thinly sliced red onion.

Prepare the Dressing:

Whisk Dressing:
- In a small bowl, whisk together extra-virgin olive oil, apple cider vinegar, honey, Dijon mustard, salt, and black pepper until well combined.

Toss Salad with Dressing:

- Drizzle the dressing over the salad and gently toss to coat all the ingredients evenly.

Serve:
- Transfer the Washington Apple Walnut Salad to individual serving plates or a large platter.

Garnish:
- If desired, garnish the salad with additional crumbled feta cheese and a sprinkle of toasted walnuts.

Enjoy:
- Serve immediately and enjoy the vibrant flavors of this Washington-inspired salad!

This salad captures the essence of Washington's delicious apples and pairs them with the satisfying crunch of walnuts and the sweetness of grapes. The combination of flavors and textures makes it a delightful and nutritious dish. Enjoy!

Idaho Sage and Honey Glazed Chicken (Idaho)

Ingredients:

- 4 bone-in, skin-on chicken thighs
- Salt and black pepper, to taste
- 2 tablespoons olive oil
- 1/4 cup fresh sage leaves, chopped
- 1/4 cup honey
- 2 tablespoons Dijon mustard
- 2 cloves garlic, minced
- 1/2 cup chicken broth
- Zest of 1 lemon
- 1 tablespoon lemon juice
- Lemon wedges and additional fresh sage for garnish (optional)

Instructions:

Preheat Oven:
- Preheat your oven to 375°F (190°C).

Season Chicken:
- Season the chicken thighs with salt and black pepper on both sides.

Sear Chicken:
- In an oven-safe skillet, heat olive oil over medium-high heat. Sear the chicken thighs, skin-side down, until golden brown. Flip and sear the other side. Remove excess fat if necessary.

Add Sage:
- Add chopped sage to the skillet and cook for about a minute until fragrant.

Prepare Glaze:
- In a small bowl, whisk together honey, Dijon mustard, minced garlic, chicken broth, lemon zest, and lemon juice.

Coat Chicken:
- Pour the honey and sage glaze over the seared chicken thighs, making sure they are well coated.

Bake:
- Transfer the skillet to the preheated oven and bake for about 25-30 minutes or until the chicken reaches an internal temperature of 165°F (74°C) and the skin is crispy.

Baste Chicken:
- Baste the chicken with the glaze halfway through the cooking time.

Serve:
- Once the chicken is cooked through and has a beautiful glaze, remove it from the oven.

Garnish (Optional):
- Garnish with lemon wedges and additional fresh sage if desired.

Rest and Enjoy:
- Allow the chicken to rest for a few minutes before serving. Spoon some of the delicious sage and honey glaze over each piece when serving.

Enjoy:
- Enjoy the delightful flavors of this Idaho Sage and Honey Glazed Chicken with the perfect balance of sweetness and savory herbiness!

This dish celebrates the flavors of Idaho with a simple yet flavorful combination of sage and honey, creating a delicious glaze for the chicken. Serve it with your favorite sides for a complete and satisfying meal!

Oregon Marionberry BBQ Pulled Pork Sliders (Oregon)

Ingredients:

For the Pulled Pork:

- 3-4 lbs pork shoulder or pork butt, trimmed
- Salt and black pepper, to taste
- 1 tablespoon smoked paprika
- 1 tablespoon onion powder
- 1 tablespoon garlic powder
- 1 teaspoon cumin
- 1 teaspoon dried thyme
- 1 onion, sliced
- 4 cloves garlic, minced
- 1 cup chicken broth

For the Marionberry BBQ Sauce:

- 1 cup marionberry preserves
- 1/2 cup ketchup
- 1/4 cup apple cider vinegar
- 2 tablespoons Dijon mustard
- 1 tablespoon Worcestershire sauce
- 1 teaspoon smoked paprika
- Salt and black pepper, to taste

For Sliders:

- Slider buns
- Coleslaw (optional, for topping)
- Pickles (optional, for serving)

Instructions:

Prepare the Pulled Pork:

    Preheat Oven:
- Preheat your oven to 300°F (150°C).

    Season Pork:

- Season the pork shoulder with salt, black pepper, smoked paprika, onion powder, garlic powder, cumin, and dried thyme. Rub the seasonings into the meat.

Sear Pork:
- In an oven-safe pot or Dutch oven, heat a bit of oil over medium-high heat. Sear the pork on all sides until it's browned.

Add Aromatics:
- Add sliced onion and minced garlic to the pot. Cook for a few minutes until the onions are softened.

Add Broth:
- Pour in chicken broth, cover the pot, and transfer it to the preheated oven.

Slow Cook:
- Slow cook the pork in the oven for about 3-4 hours, or until it's tender and easily pulls apart with a fork.

Shred Pork:
- Remove the pork from the pot and shred it using two forks. Discard any excess fat.

Prepare the Marionberry BBQ Sauce:

Combine Ingredients:
- In a saucepan, combine marionberry preserves, ketchup, apple cider vinegar, Dijon mustard, Worcestershire sauce, smoked paprika, salt, and black pepper.

Simmer Sauce:
- Simmer the sauce over medium heat, stirring occasionally, until it thickens and becomes a flavorful barbecue sauce.

Mix with Pulled Pork:
- Mix the shredded pork with the marionberry BBQ sauce until well coated.

Assemble Sliders:

Toast Buns:
- Optionally, toast the slider buns.

Top with Pulled Pork:
- Place a generous portion of the marionberry BBQ pulled pork onto each slider bun.

Add Extras:
- Top with coleslaw and pickles if desired.

Serve and Enjoy:
- Serve the Oregon Marionberry BBQ Pulled Pork Sliders and savor the delicious combination of savory pulled pork with the unique sweetness of marionberries!

These sliders showcase the regional flavor of Oregon with the addition of marionberry BBQ sauce, creating a delightful twist on the classic pulled pork sandwich. Enjoy!

Montana Huckleberry Cheesecake Bars (Montana)

Ingredients:

For the Crust:

- 1 1/2 cups graham cracker crumbs
- 1/2 cup unsalted butter, melted
- 1/4 cup granulated sugar

For the Cheesecake Filling:

- 16 oz (2 blocks) cream cheese, softened
- 1/2 cup granulated sugar
- 2 large eggs
- 1 teaspoon vanilla extract
- 1/4 cup all-purpose flour
- 1/2 cup sour cream
- 1 cup fresh or frozen huckleberries

For the Huckleberry Topping:

- 1 cup fresh or frozen huckleberries
- 1/4 cup granulated sugar
- 1 tablespoon lemon juice
- 1 tablespoon water
- 1 tablespoon cornstarch (optional, for thickening)

Instructions:

Prepare the Crust:

Preheat Oven:
- Preheat your oven to 325°F (163°C). Line a 9x9-inch baking pan with parchment paper, leaving an overhang for easy removal.

Make Crust:
- In a bowl, combine graham cracker crumbs, melted butter, and granulated sugar. Press the mixture into the bottom of the prepared pan to form an even crust.

Bake Crust:

- Bake the crust in the preheated oven for 10 minutes. Remove and let it cool slightly.

Prepare the Cheesecake Filling:

Make Cheesecake Batter:
- In a large mixing bowl, beat the softened cream cheese until smooth. Add sugar and continue beating until well combined. Mix in eggs, one at a time, followed by vanilla extract. Add flour and sour cream, mixing until smooth.

Fold in Huckleberries:
- Gently fold in the huckleberries until evenly distributed throughout the cheesecake batter.

Pour Over Crust:
- Pour the cheesecake batter over the baked crust, spreading it into an even layer.

Bake Cheesecake:
- Bake in the oven for about 35-40 minutes, or until the center is set and the edges are lightly golden.

Prepare the Huckleberry Topping:

Cook Huckleberry Sauce:
- In a saucepan, combine huckleberries, sugar, lemon juice, and water. Cook over medium heat until the huckleberries release their juices and the mixture thickens slightly. If desired, mix in cornstarch dissolved in a little water to thicken the sauce.

Cool and Top Cheesecake:
- Let the huckleberry sauce cool, then spread it over the baked cheesecake layer.

Chill:
- Refrigerate the cheesecake bars for at least 4 hours, or preferably overnight, to set.

Slice and Serve:
- Once chilled, lift the cheesecake out of the pan using the parchment paper overhang. Slice into bars and serve.

Enjoy:
- Enjoy the luscious Montana Huckleberry Cheesecake Bars, a perfect blend of creamy cheesecake and the unique flavor of huckleberries!

These bars are a delightful way to showcase the deliciousness of Montana's huckleberries in a classic cheesecake form. Perfect for any occasion!

www.ingramcontent.com/pod-product-compliance
Lightning Source LLC
LaVergne TN
LVHW081605060526
838201LV00054B/2088